Into the Dark Cloud

Sons Arise! Volume Two

Mike Parsons

Into the Dark Cloud
Sons Arise! Volume Two

Copyright © 2024 Mike Parsons,
Freedom Apostolic Ministries Ltd.

Cover Design: Jeremy Westcott.
Copyright © 2024 Jeremy Westcott,
Freedom Apostolic Ministries Ltd.

The right of Mike Parsons to be identified as the author of this work has been asserted by him in accordance with the Copyright, Designs and Patents Act 1988.

All rights reserved. No part of this publication may be reproduced or transmitted in any form or by any means, electronic or mechanical including photocopying, recording or any information storage or retrieval system, without prior permission in writing from the publishers.

First published in the United Kingdom in 2024 by
The Choir Press
in conjunction with
Freedom Apostolic Ministries Ltd.

ISBN 978-1-78963-438-9

Contents

Introduction to Sons Arise!..v
1. The Dark Cloud 7
2. An Open Heaven..19
3. Fatherhood and sonship 34
4. Healing Father Wounds 54
5. Communion 62
6. Redemptive Gifts 76
7. The Dance Floor 90
8. The Soaking Room 104
9. The Fire of Transformation 120
10. The Judgment Seat..129
11. Will You Marry Me? 136
12. Writing Your Ketubah 158
13. My Dark Cloud Testimony 171
14. Preparing the soul..187
15. Separating and Reintegrating Soul and Spirit 210
16. The Bridal Chamber 228
Further resources 235
Scripture quotations 236

*For the anxious longing of the creation waits eagerly
for the revealing of the sons of God.*
(Romans 8:19).

*"Arise, shine; for your light has come,
And the glory of the Lord has risen upon you."*
(Isaiah 60:1).

*He made darkness His hiding place,
His canopy around Him,
Darkness of waters, thick clouds of the skies.*
(Psalm 18:11).

Introduction to Sons Arise!

Several years ago, I had an experience in which God took me out into the solar system and showed me a picture of the world spinning. As I looked, it stopped and I saw arcs of blue light all over the globe, a little like this image:

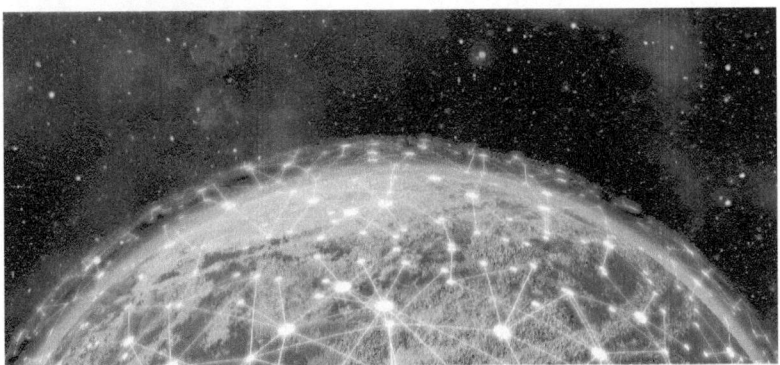

He told me that He was (and is) calling people to connect and become engaged in sonship, especially in the governmental aspect of sonship; and that these arcs were a representation of all the interactions going on around the world, interactions that I was going to connect with. At that point, I did not really know anyone around the world, so when God said "I want you to connect with people around the world," inside I was thinking "How? I don't know anybody!"

But whenever you say 'yes' to God, He finds a way. So I said 'yes' and since then this has become an outworked picture for me, as I have connected up with people across many different continents (both in person and via the internet) and in many different settings, including the six original 'Sons Arise!' conferences and intensives and the three 'Restoration of all Things' events.

This book, together with the previous one and the remaining volumes which are intended to make up this series, is a continuation of this outworking.

1. The Dark Cloud

"Into the Dark Cloud" may seem quite a cryptic title, but hopefully by the end of this book you will have found out for yourself what that dark cloud is and how to engage it.

A process of transformation

For me the dark cloud describes a process of transformation and metamorphosis. For example, think of how a caterpillar becomes a butterfly. Sometimes God places us in a cocoon to isolate us from the world in order to transform our lives. I do not know where you are in your journey with God, but if you are serious about allowing Him to transform you, you can view this book as an opportunity to engage that metamorphosis. This is the second book in the *Sons Arise!* series, and it would certainly be a good idea to read the first book[1] (or listen to the recordings of the *Engaging the Father* conference) before embarking on this one; but wherever you are, God will meet you, and that is the key. We do not need to compare ourselves with anyone else: our journey is unique and we are all uniquely made. We are all on a path to engage God more fully, as well as our personal destiny and sonship.

So in the activations and engagements we will do together, I encourage you to embrace what you can embrace and go with the flow without over-analysing what is going on. If you try too hard to dissect everything you may interrupt the flow, so just allow what happens to happen. It will not always be cognitive, and you may be unaware of exactly what God is doing. Do not be concerned about that, your spirit will receive even if your soul is not able to.

That has happened to me over and over again: I would have an encounter with God, I would not know what it did, I would just accept the reality that it did something; when I looked back in hindsight I could see what had happened and often how it had triggered a season of transformation in my life.

---

[1] For details please visit eg.freedomarc.org/books

Some of these times of encounter may be a trigger for you, and my desire is that you will get whatever God desires you to get. Allow Him to take over this process, because sometimes we think we are coming for one thing but He has a completely different agenda. In *Engaging the Father* I shared the story of how I went to a seminar on establishing social businesses and ended up walking on a beach with Jesus; so I have learned that it is always best to go with the flow of His agenda, not dismiss or resist it.

I did initially resist engaging the dark cloud because I did not understand it, and at that time I did not think I could cooperate with something I did not understand. I will share more of that in a later chapter. But now I have come to accept that I do not need to understand everything (or even anything): if I am cooperating, what my spirit receives will eventually be released into my life.

The Person of God

He made darkness His hiding place, His canopy around Him, Darkness of waters, thick clouds of the skies (Psalm 18:11).

God's presence is here with us. Heaven is open and where two or three are gathered (not only physically, but in the spirit) His presence is here. He dwells with us and within us by His Spirit. But His person dwells within what is often described in scripture as a dark cloud (the verse above from Psalm 18 is just one example). So there is a difference between engaging His presence and engaging His person in a face-to-face type encounter.

We will look to do that later in this book, and you may well be able to engage it by then; however, if you are not yet ready, God will meet with you however you can. He has a purpose and a plan for everyone reading this: just go with what that plan is. If you are proactive and willing to pursue the dark cloud experience, that time frame can be accelerated; and at the time that is right for you, you will be ready.

Whenever I introduce people to this and share my testimony with them, I always encourage them to surrender early in the process rather than at the end. Acceleration is always possible because when we engage in the presence of God and in the heavens we are outside of the normal, local time constraints of this earthly realm. Time still exists in heaven, but it operates differently in every realm. I have learned to frame time for my life in this physical realm, but when I am in the realms of heaven, God can do things in an hour that would sometimes take a month or a year here. In the heavens, our spirit is not subject to the same limitations; therefore things appear accelerated from our point of view, although it is actually still a process we have gone through in heavenly time. Even growth in maturity can be accelerated to some degree. And even if we might not always be aware of what is happening in those heavenly engagements, we can still experience the fruit of them in our earthly lives.

Embrace the testimony

I will begin by sharing some of my testimony. As a forerunner, God has called me to open a window of opportunity for others. You can follow your own path through that doorway, that portal, but you can know that it is open for you by taking whatever God has done for me and applying that to your own situation. Simply say, "I receive that testimony and I ask You, God, to do that in my life the way You want to do it." Note that, the way He wants to do it: you cannot copy someone else's testimony. Be open for your own experience; embrace the testimony as revealing potential for you.

We have a mountain of authority here at Freedom, and our mandate is to gather, connect, impart and release. By one means or another we gather people and connect with them around the globe. I mentor people worldwide from my home or office, and although they may not be physically here with us, we have connection. In a sense this book, too, can be a means whereby that gathering takes place. And we really want to connect people with God, at a different level than they have done before; and to pursue that as a lifestyle. So for everyone reading this, we want to impart the desire and capacity to receive revelation and experiential truth.

Every time I teach, I warn people not to believe anything I say just because I say it. Yes, I am saying it because it is my experience and my testimony; and I believe it is true. I do not share theory: everything I am writing is from personal experience and I know there is reality to it. But you need to have your own experience. You need to have God speak to you and reveal things to you because otherwise it is just information. There is value in information if it leads you into revelation, but your own revelation is essential. In every testimony I share, it is my intention to activate your potential and ability to have that experience; and in that process God will speak to you however He wants.

Continual challenge

I love the way God interacts with people, because He speaks to us all differently to get the truth over to us. When we try to share the truth with someone else, sometimes we use language which makes that truth hard for them to access. When God speaks to us, He always uses suitable language and speaks in a way we will be able to connect with. That is not to say that it will always be easy for us to accept or understand, as in my experience He often deliberately says things which challenge preconceived ideas about Him.

In fact my journey has been made up of continual challenge of what I thought I knew, until I finally realised that most of what I thought I knew was not true at all, particularly my idea of what God is like. My image of Him was based in what I was taught and took on board from being around Christian churches and ministries for most of my life. I absorbed a lot of what I thought were truths from the various streams I was involved with: Methodist, Brethren, and charismatic. All had particular ways of thinking and believing, most of which I never really thought about but just accepted. God started to challenge what had taken me half a century to accumulate.

So when you meet with God, what He reveals may be surprising: do not be shocked or put off by that and do not fight it. If you are struggling with something He shares or something that He challenges you over, ask Him to affirm it: do not get defensive with God. I did, and I can tell you, it will do you no good. I had 'does not compute!' lights flashing in my mind and went through a very painful stage of cognitive dissonance because my encounters were revealing truth that did not match up with my entrenched beliefs.

Have you been taught that in those circumstances you should always go with your beliefs because you cannot trust your experience, that experience is subjective? Look again at the Bible, which is what we are often told we should use as a reference point for our experiences. What is the Bible but multiple accounts of people's subjective experiences with God? Everyone from Adam in Genesis to John in Revelation had an encounter with God, not a theory about Him. All the way through, those people had experiences of Him which shaped their lives and their stories. Now we read what they wrote and we take it as the letter of the law. Honestly, when we have experiences and write them down, they become as real as anything they wrote in the Bible, because they too were writing out of experience.

God spoke to them, they had an encounter, or they had a vision. Theirs are remarkable stories of how God interacted with them, which sometimes challenged their beliefs. Take Gideon for instance, hiding away in the wine press when the angel of the Lord came and said "You mighty man of valour!" Gideon was looking around thinking "Who's that angel talking to? Because it can't be me..." But God knew better. God knew his destiny and called it forth in this encounter with the angel. So if you encounter angels, it can be life-changing: they are messengers, and their message will likely provoke some kind of reaction. Expect that type of encounter: do not fight it but lay hold of it and find out how it applies to your life. And ask God about it, so that you are not leaning to your own understanding of your encounters, as I used to.

I shared in *Engaging the Father* how I had a series of encounters in a secret place of intimacy with Him. It had a little bench and a tree swing, and I thought it was a little bit of heaven just for me. It turned out to be the garden of my heart, which I have since learned how to cultivate. One day I was there with the Father and he showed me a huge tapestry hanging from the branches of the trees. Woven into the tapestry were pictures of all my encounters with God over the years, all incredibly detailed. As I looked, I re-encountered the experience each image represented: that is how real it was. I completely forgot that the Father was with me because I was so absorbed with what I was looking at.

Then, right in the middle, I saw a tiny thread and thought, "I wonder, if I follow this little thread, where is it going to take me?" So I pulled the thread. When I was growing up and I had a loose thread in my jumper, my mum always told me, "Don't pull the thread." I did not listen to her then, and I did not follow her advice now. When I pulled the thread, the whole tapestry unravelled in front of me onto the ground. Standing behind it was the Father, laughing! He said "What have you been looking at? What is this amazing image that you have been viewing? What is an image of Me called?"

And it suddenly struck me, it was an idol. That is what images are, they are idols. And all the marvellous encounters I had had in heaven over six or seven years had become my understanding of God: but an understanding still shaped by my belief systems. As I say, we are not supposed to lean to our own understanding. Even in our encounters with God there needs to be an ongoing life-giving relationship. So I stopped trying to form an understanding: I have decided that I just want a relationship with God every day, one in which I can walk with Him and He is walking with me in intimacy, and therefore I do not need to understand.

So now, when He says He would like me to do this or that, or when He shows me something, I am not trying to analyse it, figure it out or work it out in order to create a new belief system around it. If I did, He would have to demolish it again because it would be limited by the capacity of my mind; and although my mind is expanding with the encounters I am having, it is still limited compared to the mind of Christ. What I have come to know of God in all these encounters is a fraction of a fraction of the infiniteness of God. If I think that my mind is capable of creating an accurate, complete view of God which I can understand, I am only deceiving myself. So I have given up trying. Now I just want the ongoing relationship and encounters that reveal who God actually is.

It took me the best part of eighteen months to have all my 'views of God' deconstructed in my mind (or as many as I became aware of – and I may still have more, because this is an ongoing process) so that my relationship and my encounters with Him could begin to reveal the truth of who He really is, without being framed by those misconceptions. The Bible is there to point us to a relationship with God, not to be the substance of it. As much as I love the fact that it records inspiring clues which give me insight into what is possible for me, and so becomes a doorway for me to engage; yet the extent of my engagement with Him will go far beyond what could ever be contained within a book (even if that book is the Bible). And remember, the book itself says that if all that Jesus did was put into books, the world would not be big enough to contain them.

So I encourage you to go with the encounter and allow the Spirit of God in you, the Spirit of Truth, to affirm that encounter. Do not only use what is in the Bible to affirm it, because some of what you may encounter will not be in there. You may think, "my experience must never contradict the Bible." That may be all very well, but it might still contradict your understanding of what the Bible says. I had a real problem with this until I realised that it was my understanding of the Bible that did not line up with what I was experiencing.

I had to ask God about it, because I was very concerned; having been a Bible Methodist and a Brethren 'Word' person. I knew very well that some of my experiences were outside of – and some even seemed to conflict with – what I believed the Bible said about the subject. "How do I know that these are actual genuine encounters with You?" And He answered, "Doesn't the Bible say that if you ask the Father for something good He'll give it you, not something bad?" Well, that gave me a Bible text, for which I was grateful. He added "Use love as your measure. If it is love, it is Me. If it is not love, it is not Me."

So now I had another problem. What about all the love I see that is outside of what I would have previously seen as being 'God'? How does that work? Eventually I came to understand that God is at work in everybody; we are all made in His image and everyone is a child of God, whether they know the reality of that in relationship yet or not. He desires a relationship with all of them, so He is at work in them to help them discover that relationship with Him. So when someone loves their children, that love is an expression of God because they are made in God's image to love their children like He loves His children.

If you struggle with anything I am saying, or anything you receive in your encounters, I would encourage you to allow God to reveal the truth: go back to the Father and ask Him to reveal Himself in and through whatever you are struggling with. Sometimes He uses the trials and struggles to transform us – He certainly does with me.

Activations

As you read this book, take the opportunity to find time and space in which to engage God as Father in intimacy as His son or daughter. The activations that I present are just little sound bites, opportunities to taste and see; you will have to go back into them yourself, perhaps several times, to let those experiences become a lifestyle. Whilst I will offer suggestions of what you might wish to do during an activation, if you sense that Jesus wants to take you elsewhere or to do something different please feel free to go with that instead. He is quite capable of engaging each of us in a very individual way, so that what each of us experiences in the course of an activation will be unique.

In each case you can, if you wish, choose to follow the text of the activation as it appears in the book, but since most of them start by suggesting you close your eyes, we have made recorded audio versions available for you too. You can access these through links on the document you will find at freedomarc.org/itdc-resources or by scanning the QR code (right) with your phone camera. Also throughout the book you will see a unique QR code at the head of each activation, which you can scan to stream the audio just for that exercise.

Scan the QR code above to find some additional resources

In some of them, if you listen to the audio, you will hear certain sounds and frequencies which we use to help open up our subconscious and some of our blind-self areas. We use crystal singing bowls, which produce a resonant frequency that can engage beyond the limitations of our conscious mind, and background music which has been composed and recorded for this specific purpose.

Just relax and allow the frequencies to come around you. Allow your spirit, soul and body to be surrounded with the sound of God's voice which is carried on that frequency. When someone writes or performs music with creative intention, that intention is present in the music. For example, when I play the piece called 'Restoration Through Harmony', my intention agrees with that of the composer and performer, which is for restoration to take place as that music is played. You can choose to engage it and to receive that intention or you can just hear it as background music.

When we do activations in a live setting we often also diffuse fragrances of essential oils – if you are familiar with essential oils and would like to do that at home, please do. Some people look at all this and dismiss it as 'new age' but there is sound science behind it. If you are uncomfortable with it in theory, by all means ask God about it for yourself. If you use our audio and are uncomfortable with it in practice, I would encourage you to persevere: sometimes that discomfort is caused by the depth to which these frequencies reach into our soul.

As I say, the purpose of these guided engagements is to develop a lifestyle. In my journey I had to practise to hear God's voice (because I could not hear Him); then I had to practise to see in the spirit (because I could not do that either). Then after I engaged heaven the first time, involuntarily, I had to practise what God showed me to do because I did not know how to get back there. I practised these things every day, over and over again. Nowadays I do not need to practise them anymore, and I no longer need to do 'activations' in my own life, because engaging with God and with the heavenly realms has become my lifestyle. I engage God every day and journal those encounters. I really love listening to Him and He shares His heart with me.

That is my testimony. If you want a deeper relationship with God for yourself, and if you really desire sonship, you will have to pursue it. It will not just fall into your lap. At times God will give you something to inspire you or encourage you and sometimes they may be completely unexpected (like my involuntary engagement with heaven – I was sitting at my desk when a portal opened and suddenly I was in heaven). But God showed me that was possible in order to give me the option to pursue it. I could have settled for an occasional supernatural encounter every now and again but I really wanted to develop it into a lifestyle.

It was not easy, even to get started. The next day I sat at my desk again waiting for the portal to open. I tried for two years to get that portal to open, without success. Nothing worked, not one thing I tried. They might work for others; they did not work for me, because God had a different process for me to go through. Eventually I got to the point of saying "Okay, God, if You want this then it's over to You now." I have got to that stage a number of times in my life – not giving up on the desire – just realising that I was coming to the end of what I could do. If I had come to that realisation earlier, perhaps it would not have taken two years before God took me back into that realm and then taught me how to stay in there or go in and out at will.

Relational, not formulaic

What the Father wanted to show me was that everything with Him is relational, not formulaic. So if anyone offers you a formula, I suggest you treat it cautiously because it may be something from God which works for them but when they export it (or try to franchise it), it really does not work as regularly or effectively for other people. Everything in the kingdom is relational, and you need to find your own way in it that works for you. That is why times of personal reflection while you are reading this will be key to your engaging with God and finding what He wants for you, rather than anything I might write or say.

We will be looking at redemptive gifts (and there is a survey which may help you identify what your particular gift is, if you have not done that) reflecting on who He has made you to be, how He wired you as a person and how that might have been affected by the world in which you live. He wants to bring you back to that, but when He does, it is because He wants you to surrender it to Him. I discovered that I was getting my identity from doing, (even though I was doing things which were in line with my redemptive gift) rather than learning how to just be. There is nothing wrong in doing all the things that God wants us to do but if we are doing them to give us our identity (rather than knowing our identity first, and then doing), we have it the wrong way around. He wants us all to come to the point where we can surrender who He made us to be so that He can empower who we are. When we live that way, everything changes.

Night watch

I have legislated for an opening of the night watch, for you to experience restoration of your soul in the garden of rest at night. Many of you will be reading this just before you go to sleep. As you close your eyes, engage the garden of your heart and rest there. If you do not know what that is, just make a choice: "I am sending my soul into the garden of my heart to rest. As I sleep, my spirit is going to be actively working with God in the process of transforming my life." In that way you can benefit from eight hours or so of Him working with you on all He has been doing during the day and continuing the process of outworking it in your life. You do not need to be conscious for God to work, you can trust Him and engage by faith.

Faith of the Son of God

People often tell me that they are just doing all this by faith, as if that is a bad thing, substandard or unsatisfactory. God always responds to faith and He gives us the faith to respond: it is His faith we are living by, not our own:

I am crucified with Christ: nevertheless I live; yet not I, but Christ liveth in me: and the life which I now live in the flesh I live by the faith of the Son of God, who loved me, and gave himself for me (Galatians 2:20 KJV).

Does your version of the Bible say 'faith *in* the Son of God'? Nearly all do. But for once, the King James has it right. Here is a literal translation (harder to read but it makes the point):

with Christ I have been crucified, and live no more do I, and Christ doth live in me; and that which I now live in the flesh - in the faith I live of the Son of God, who did love me and did give himself for me (Galatians 2:20 YLT).

We do not have to drum up enough belief to make something happen: we just have to (by His grace) receive His faith to believe and then allow it to happen. Let's not get into 'dead works' by trying to make something happen that God has already done and which He wants to reveal to us so that we can experience it.

2. An Open Heaven

We have also legislated for the environment around this *Sons Arise!* teaching to be a safe place for you to explore and to go into whatever depth God wants to take you. There is an open heaven over us, and we invite heaven's representatives to be here with you as you read and engage.

The four faces of God will manifest for you: they reflect something of God's heart and His government in sonship that can be transformational. You may get to see through the eyes of the eagle and perceive yourself from that perspective; or the eyes of the lion, the ox or the man. Such encounters can give us insight we would not get anywhere else.

There are four angels of transition (in fact they are orders of angels) that God has given us for the seasons that we are in. Take the opportunity to engage with them. Transformation, Winds of Change, Sound of Many Waters and Refiner's Fire come to help us mature into sonship. When you are in a time of reflection, you might invite Winds of Change to come and bring you into a new season, or Sound of Many Waters to bring the resonant frequency of God's voice, calling you into your destiny. They are not limited by geography, so you can engage with them anywhere and at any time you choose.

The men in white linen, the cloud of witnesses, are also here surrounding us, and can interact with us at times to help us. One or more of them may be particularly assigned to us because of our destiny, and when they connect to us they have insight to impart (whether cognitively or not).

There are gathering angels too: you can read about them in Matthew 13. They are quite fierce, in my experience, rather stern-looking, but they have a purpose in gathering and removing stumbling blocks and lawlessness, not out of the world but out of the kingdom that is within us. Stumbling blocks are hindrances to you coming into maturity: when you surrender, the gathering angels can remove obstacles that would cause you to stumble, so embrace that when it happens.

As you are reading you may find that you sense some of these beings around you or engaging you: whether angels or one or more of the cloud of witnesses. Again do not try to analyse it, but just relax. "Father, if you have sent a gathering angel to gather a stumbling block out of my life, or if you have sent one of the cloud of witnesses, I am open to whatever You are doing." Your choice to have such an attitude of surrender and openness enables your engagements to be much more fruitful.

Trauma

In those times, allow peace to fill the atmosphere around you so that healing and wholeness can come. Allow joy to fill the atmosphere so that you can be brought to a place of strength. The joy of the Lord is our strength and when we are whole, we are strong; when we are fragmented we are weak. If you are fragmented into 25 parts, you are going to feel 1/25th of who you could be, because each one of those parts will be draining away the energy of your life. We learned Lie Busting from Jonathan Cavan, and there is a section of that process called a 'parts scan,' looking to identify whether parts of you are emotionally stuck at particular ages of your life, and if you are dissociated through trauma.

I never considered the possibility of dissociation in me, because I thought I was all right (as we often do). Then several years ago, I reacted to a situation regarding my grandchildren in a way that was completely out of proportion and I realised I had been triggered by something. I had no idea where it came from. I had to deal with the aftermath of my behaviour and apologise to those concerned, and then I asked God to show me what had triggered me. All I could see was an area of darkness. I could not penetrate it. I tried everything I knew to penetrate that darkness and discover what it was. I had no idea that there was a part of me that was stuck in darkness, and that the situation had triggered this stuck part of me to come to the surface and behave like a child.

My grandchildren were unharmed, but my perception was that they had been in danger and something could have happened to them because (as I saw it) they were not being properly supervised. Even though I knew they were in fact safe, it was this fear for them that triggered my behaviour. In walking through this with God, He was able to show me that I had a traumatic experience as a seven year old child in which I was abducted at a country show. It was so traumatic that I dissociated it. My sister was also abducted, and I remembered that she had got lost, but that was my only memory of the day.

That trauma created a part of me which got stuck and, as that was the only occasion it ever triggered in my life, I had no idea it was there. God allowed the trigger for it to come to the surface and for me to be healed. For fifty years of my life I was unaware of it, so there is a possibility there may be something in your life you do not know about either, draining your energy and causing you to be less than you really are.

In chapter 14 we will do a parts scan and look at how we can allow God to identify any of those issues and bring us into wholeness. It does not have to be complicated. When I discovered that I was dissociated, I enquired of God what to do. He asked me, "Do you want to come into wholeness?" I said "Yes" and He said "Come to me, then." It was a very simple process but I had to feel safe to come to Him, or that part would not have surfaced and I would not have become integrated and made whole.

Jesus is a safe place. The Father is a safe place. But if your natural father was responsible for your trauma, or if you hold him responsible, you might find it harder to see God as a safe place. That happened with me, because of my experience with my earthly father. Only when Jesus pointed out to me that I needed to engage the Father was I able to face that truth and have my father wound healed by His love.

Rest

"Come to Me, all who are weary and heavy-laden, and I will give you rest. Take My yoke upon you and learn from Me, for I am gentle and humble in heart, and you will find rest for your

souls. For My yoke is easy and My burden is light." (Matthew 11:28-30).

It is important that we do not strive but are in rest. As soon as we are striving, we are trying to do something or get something. Yoke yourself to Jesus. The place of rest is the place of surrender to Him, yoked to Him in relationship. Not striving, not analysing, and not studying: it is by choice, not willpower. You can make a choice based on the desire of your heart; if you try to put your willpower into action, you will just be using the power of your soul.

God will reveal the truth of who we are and bring us to that place where we find rest in Him. We make a choice to surrender. Some people will say that you need to die, not just surrender. Well, I have good news for you: you are already dead! You were co-crucified with Christ. You do need to identify with that and to experience it by surrendering, but do not try to die. For years I tried to die every day. I thought that as a living sacrifice, I needed to die. But the clue is in the title: a 'living' sacrifice, not a dead one.

Eventually I got it: I already died with Him on the cross. I have been crucified with Him. I do not need to try to die, I need to surrender to His death and to identify with His life and His resurrection. He did not stay dead, which is awesome; He made everything alive, including us. Now we can enter into the resurrection life by identifying with the fact that in the cross we have everything that is available for us. We come into a finished work. He finished it: it is done; we come into it, we experience it, and it transforms us.

I do not believe that it all happens automatically. When we began to follow Christ we did not immediately experience complete physical, emotional, and mental wholeness. That wholeness or healing is available for us, but only by entering into and realising what He has done. As we learn to surrender, we will find that transformation happens much more readily.

Be still, and know that I am God (Psalm 46:10a NKJV).

The NASB renders that as 'Stop striving' and its footnote says 'Let go, relax!' Let us take the opportunity to be still and allow the presence of God to move around us.

Yet those who wait for the Lord
Will gain new strength;
They will mount up with wings like eagles,
They will run and not get tired,
They will walk and not become weary
(Isaiah 40:31).

One aspect of 'waiting for the Lord' is not trying to run ahead of Him. We want to allow Him to set the pace, and to journey with Him without either racing ahead or lagging behind, just walking along together in relationship.

Be transformed

If we want to operate from the identity of who God created us to be rather than from how our soul has been affected by life, then we will need to be aware of the three likely sources of those effects: nature, nurture and trauma.

Nature: all that has been handed down to us genetically by our natural parents.

Nurture: how we have learned (or been taught) to function in this world.

Trauma: the consequences of things that have happened to us.

All three contribute to how we live, but now God wants to free us from them so that we can live according to who He says we are and who He created us to be. First we need to put an end to religious dead works: all the things that anyone says that you can do to make this happen. There is nothing you can 'do'. But as you surrender to the Father in relationship, He can make it happen. Only He can transform us: we cannot transform ourselves.

And do not be conformed to this world, but be transformed by the renewing of your mind, so that you may prove what the will of God is, that which is good and acceptable and perfect (Romans 12:2).

We cannot even renew our own minds. I thought that scripture said we had to (look again: it does not). So I tried for 50 years to renew my mind. I memorised scriptures, quoted scriptures and positively confessed scriptures because I was taught that would do it. I learned a lot of the Bible that way; I have all that scripture in me (and now it flows effortlessly out of me) but it never actually renewed my mind. Only God can renew our minds because He is the truth. He renews our minds by encountering us with that truth which changes us.

"...and you will know the truth, and the truth will set you free." (John 8:32)

Only the truth that you know will set you free. How are we going to know the truth? Not by reading someone else's book or doing someone else's course. Not even mine. What that can do is stimulate us to find it for ourselves by engaging God, who will reveal the truth to each of us so that we can live in it.

Desire, discipline, delight

So when this book gets into some tough areas, please do not tune out, switch off or walk away. If it gets difficult, surrender to God. Again, I am not saying that you have to take my word for anything: be still and wait in rest, and see if He has something to say to you about it.

That was the process God took me through: learning to be still and wait in rest. For two years I had loved being still, waiting and resting; until He told me to, and then I could not do it anymore. That sometimes happens because it challenges the whole dynamic of what works for us! Generally it is our soul becoming uncomfortable in facing what it needs to face.

I went through various stages and processes of transformation, such as dealing with trading floors in my own heart, its motivations, thoughts and intentions. It was not at all pleasant for my soul because I had to admit that I was not very nice in some ways, and that my motivation was often not entirely pure. It was not easy, but because I knew the love of God it enabled me to trust Him, so instead of becoming defensive, I learned to surrender. It was horrible to think that I was really like that: that my motives really were driven by my soul's need or desire. But I realised that God loved me anyway so I was able to let it go. If I had gone with my feelings I would have stopped right there and never made it through to transformation. If you get to a crisis point, try not to back off.

Personal desire and pursuit will take you through the discipline to the delight. Stick with it. It can require fortitude and discipline to press on through but when you come out on the other side I can promise you it will have been worth it.

Jesus has made a way

Jesus has made a way. He is the door. He has torn the veil. We can enter into all that was finished on the cross and the fullness of everything that He has done because He has made the way. He has opened the way for us all to experience the green pasture that we need (which is different for each of us). We have to come to a realisation of the power of the cross in our co-crucifixion, our co-resurrection and our co-ascension. All those things have been done for us and we are seated in heavenly places, even if we do not yet know it.

For the creation was subjected to futility, not willingly, but because of Him who subjected it, in hope that the creation itself also will be set free from its slavery to corruption into the freedom of the glory of the children of God. For we know that the whole creation groans and suffers the pains of childbirth together until now (Romans 8:20-22).

Our identification with the finished work of the cross will bring change to the whole of creation. Creation is waiting for the manifestation of the sons of God, the revealing of us as God's children, and it will respond to that. What is more, it is into the freedom of the glory of the children of God, into the freedom of *our* glory, that creation will be set free. I am only just discovering more of what that really means: it is beyond my natural capacity to comprehend it, but God is revealing the extent of our sonship as He reveals Himself as Father.

Intense

The manifestation of the dark cloud will envelop us with its deep, thick, intense love, peace and joy. Its darkness does not cause us to be afraid, but is a place of safety and security that cocoons us while we go through a process and brings us into a sense of the presence of God which is more powerful than anything we have experienced before. The closer you get to the centre of that cloud, the closer to the person of God; there is an intensity to be experienced the more you press into it.

Psalm 23

Here are some brief thoughts on Psalm 23, which really sums up the intimacy of my relationship with God. Engaging this psalm experientially and having encounters with the Shepherd in green pastures marked the beginning of my journey into that deeper relationship.

The Lord is my shepherd,
I shall not want.

He makes me lie down in green pastures;
He leads me beside quiet waters.
He restores my soul;
He guides me in the paths of righteousness
For His name's sake.

Even though I walk through the valley of the shadow of death,
I fear no evil, for You are with me;
Your rod and Your staff, they comfort me.
You prepare a table before me in the presence of my enemies;
You have anointed my head with oil;
My cup overflows.

Surely goodness and lovingkindness will follow me
all the days of my life,
And I will dwell in the house of the Lord forever
(Psalm 23:1-6).

- Sometimes we are so active that He has to make us lie down, otherwise He could not do anything with us.
- Notice that they are quiet waters, not stormy seas.
- It is not me that does the restoring, but Him.
- He guides me.
- 'The valley of the shadow of death' – the dark cloud may appear to be quite intimidating, but it is just a shadow for us to engage. There is no need to be afraid of allowing God to take us in there.
- His rod is comforting. It is not something to beat us up with, but to protect and guide us, to help us stay on the path and prevent us falling off the edge.
- The enemies mentioned here are not necessarily external, but can be blockages or stumbling blocks within ourselves (or possibly familiar spirits) hindering us from coming into the fullness of maturity.
- Everything we will ever need we will find on that table prepared for us. So communion, taking the body and blood of Jesus, is like a table before me (whenever I eat physical food I am looking to participate in the life of God). I see it as a picnic blanket set out in the garden, in the green pastures; I can go there at times, particularly when I am looking for things to be transformed in my life, and eat from what He has placed there for me.

Here is the same psalm in the Passion translation:

Yahweh is my best friend and my shepherd.
I always have more than enough.

He offers a resting place for me in his luxurious love.
His tracks take me to an oasis of peace
near the quiet brook of bliss.

That's where he restores and revives my life.
He opens before me the right path
and leads me along in his footsteps of righteousness
so that I can bring honor to his name.

*Even when your path takes me through
the valley of deepest darkness,
fear will never conquer me, for you already have!
Your authority is my strength and my peace.
The comfort of your love takes away my fear.
I'll never be lonely, for you are near.*

*You become my delicious feast
even when my enemies dare to fight.
You anoint me with the fragrance of your Holy Spirit;
you give me all I can drink of you until my cup overflows.*

*So why would I fear the future?
Only goodness and tender love pursue me all the days of my life.
Then afterward, when my life is through,
I'll return to your glorious presence to be forever with you!*
(Psalm 23:1-6 TPT).

We do not have to wait until we die physically of course, we have access to enter into that now. Many Christians have a covenant with death, thinking that they can only 'go to heaven' when they die. But, as we have noted, we have already died! We were co-crucified and co-resurrected.

Living and active

For the word of God is living and active and sharper than any two-edged sword, and piercing as far as the division of soul and spirit, of both joints and marrow, and able to judge the thoughts and intentions of the heart. And there is no creature hidden from His sight, but all things are open and laid bare to the eyes of Him with whom we have to do (Hebrews 4:12-13).

That living and active Word is not the Bible, in fact the letter to the Hebrews was written long before there even was a Bible anything like we know it today. Jesus is the living Word. Do not misunderstand me. God can certainly use the Bible as a sword and a living word. He has taken scriptures and given them to me, sometimes totally out of context, to speak to me and transform my life. And He can also speak scriptures to you, give you something which is totally for you in the moment, and for no-one else. But He does not limit Himself to speaking through the Bible. However He speaks to us, what is important is that it is Him speaking, and speaking to us.

Later, in chapter 15, we will invite Him to divide between soul and spirit, so that they can be reintegrated as they were intended to be, with the spirit taking the lead.

God knows everything there is to know about you, even many things you do not know about yourself, and He loves you. He loves you as much as He could possibly ever love anyone, and His love will never change. It is totally unconditional. There is nothing you can do (or not do) which will ever change His love for you.

Once we really accept the truth of that, it gives us the confidence and trust to be completely open with Him, not fearing that if we are honest with Him He will be angry or disappointed with us. He is always smiling upon us; His countenance is always fair towards us. He may be stern and fiercely opposed to whatever is robbing us, hindering us or putting stumbling blocks in our path, but never towards us. He loves us, and when we really know His love it allows us to say: "Search me, O God, and know my heart. Put me on trial and see if there's anything in me which is a hindrance and a stumbling block to me" (see Psalm 139:23-24).

In the Mirror Bible it says this:

The message God spoke to us in Christ, is the most life giving and dynamic influence in us, cutting like a surgeon's scalpel, sharper than a soldier's sword, piercing to the deepest core of human conscience, to the dividing of soul and spirit; ending the dominance of the sense realm and its neutralizing effect upon the human spirit. In this way a person's spirit is freed to become the ruling influence again in the thoughts and intentions of their heart. The scrutiny of this living Sword-Logos detects every possible disease, discerning the body's deepest secrets where joint and bone-marrow meet. (The moment we cease from our own efforts to justify ourselves, by yielding to the integrity of the message that announces the success of the Cross, God's word is triggered into action. What God spoke to us in sonship (the incarnation), radiates his image and likeness in our redeemed innocence. [Hebrews 1:1-3] This word powerfully penetrates and impacts our whole being; body, soul and spirit (Hebrews 4:12 Mirror, with translator's notes).

I would say that it can also pierce beyond the human conscience into the human subconscious, as well to the dividing of soul and spirit, so that we are not dictated to by what is around us but instead, from the inside out, we fill what is around us with the atmosphere of heaven.

We want the living word to penetrate and impact us. When God speaks to us He speaks life and truth: He opens up revelation to us. Before we can change the atmosphere around our life by flowing from the inside out, an inner transformation needs to take place. We want our spirit to be free to become the ruling influence in the thoughts and intentions of our heart, so that we are no longer ruled by our soul: the directive comes from the spirit and our soul is in complete agreement.

Our surrender, our yielding, invites and enables God's action. The whole time we are trying to do it ourselves, God is waiting for us to stop and give up. In all we are embarking upon in this book, there may be points where we have to give up. When we have been used to fighting for things all our lives or been taught that we should always be actively trying to do something, giving up is not always easy.

Hebrew marriage

But the one who joins himself to the Lord is one spirit with Him (1 Corinthians 6:17).

In order to engage the dark cloud, we are going to follow the process God took me through, the Hebrew marriage process:

- *Lakah*
- *Segullah*

- *Mikvah*
- *Ketubah*
- *Huppah*

These are linked with the four chambers of the heart:

- Garden
- Dance Floor
- Soaking Room
- Bridal Chamber

We will look at all those elements in detail, so that in the final activation you can experience your own marriage ceremony; in which you have your own vows, your own *ketubah* between you and God, and enter into a whole different level of relationship, leaving independence behind.

To close out this chapter, we will do our first activation, about being under an open heaven. God speaks to us from where He is (in eternity) to where we are in this realm, to reveal the truth from His perspective: the thoughts He has always had about each of us, the truth that He always had in mind when He made each one of us. The vast sum of those astounding thoughts are available for us to receive as He speaks into our lives.

Read through the text before closing your eyes to engage, or use the audio from the resources page. You can also scan the QR code at the head of the activation with your mobile phone to hear the recording.

We are here under an open heaven. When Jesus was under an open heaven, the Father spoke affirmation to Him. He wants to speak over us and into each one of us as His child:

- acceptance
- affirmation
- approval
- recognition
- recommendation

- commendation
- blessing
- endorsement
- validation

He has wonderful things in store for each of us, beyond what we can imagine or think; and He wants to reveal those to us in the spirit. There are things that eye has not seen and ear has not heard and the heart has never received, but they are revealed through the spirit.

Be open for Him to speak into your life.

Activation #1: Open Heaven

Close your eyes and allow the Spirit of God and the Father's voice to call to you and to speak into your spirit.

For each activation, to listen to the audio mp3 scan the QR code displayed

> Son, I call your spirit to attention
> Spirit, listen as a true son
>
> I call forth your identity as a son
> part of the Joshua generation
> the order of Melchizedek;
> I call you to enter my rest.
>
> I call you to come into deeper intimacy.
> I call you to lie down in an oasis of peace
> by the quiet brook of bliss.
>
> I call you to enter into the dark cloud of transformation.
>
> I call forth your sonship,
> your destiny, your position and your authority as a son.
> I call forth your destiny
> to manifest God's kingdom on earth as it is in heaven.
> I call forth your destiny to fill the earth with God's glory
>
> I call forth your identity, destiny and authority
> as a lord within the realms of heaven,
> as a king and as my son

to stand in the assemblies of heaven
and to experience who you have always been.

I call forth your identity and destiny.
I affirm you as My child.
I approve of you and accept you.
I pour my love
and lavish my grace, mercy and blessing upon you

You are My beloved child in whom I am well pleased,
in whom My soul delights
in whom My heart is overflowing.

I speak into your life words of affirmation,
a remembrance of the words
and thoughts within My heart that created you.

I call forth your spirit to remembrance
of who you were before you were here,
to remember the intimacy
when you stood within the circle of the dance
when you stood within the relationship
between Father, Son and Spirit.

Receive My affirmation
Receive My acceptance
Receive My approval and recognition
Receive My blessing

I speak words of remembrance from My eternal heart
deep into your spirit
that will be released into your soul.

Standing in the spirit under an open heaven, allow God to speak directly to you anything He wants to say, to reveal anything He wants to unveil.

Please stay in that place as long as you want or need.

3. Fatherhood and sonship

Relationship

One of the main keys in engaging the Father is to actually have a relationship with Him. If we are to arise as sons and come into our inheritance, our relationship with the Father is absolutely vital.

Whatever the quality of our relationship with our earthly father, it will have had an effect on our relationship with God as Father. There may be some father wounds or father issues which need healing before we can fully learn to trust the Father and go deeper into intimacy.

In this chapter I will share some of my testimony in that area and then encourage you to look at your own life, and to reflect upon your own father experiences, whether of your earthly father or your heavenly Father. Allow God to unveil and give insight into anything He wants to address. In my experience this did not happen all at once, but over years and years; in fact it is still ongoing as God continues to reveal Himself as Father in deeper and deeper ways.

In the beginning God... (Genesis 1:1).

There was a perfect relationship between the Father, Son and Spirit. They did not need anyone else: they had perfect love, joy, peace and all the other fruit of the spirit characteristic of the essence of God. But because God is love, He chose to create us from the desire of His heart. As a result, we can engage in that love, enter into a relationship with the Father, Son and Spirit, and experience the perfect love, joy and peace that exist within them. When we embrace that and reconnect with it, we encounter a level of love that surpasses anything we can find in other people.

Most of our needs in this world have been met through others. When we were young, we looked to our parents. Our mother was to take care of us, nurture us, and feed us. Our father had a role in calling forth our identity and guiding us in the right direction to help us discover who we are. Earthly parents fulfil those roles imperfectly, if at all. What is more, parents often impose their own unfulfilled expectations on their children. So in some families there is an obligation to join the family business or to continue the family line of generations of doctors or lawyers or whatever it may be. That will restrict us from being who we really are. If God has called us to be a doctor, that is awesome. But if not, and our families pressure us into that profession, we may struggle for identity. We do not know who we are because we are doing something outside our destiny. God wants us to find love, joy and peace in Him and in that place to truly discover who we are.

Engaging in love, joy and peace within the eternal heart of God has transformed my entire life. God has challenged my understanding of who He is, my mindset and my beliefs about Him. He has shown me love, love, and more love in ways I could never have imagined. At this point, all I desire is a deep relationship with Him. The way I look at and engage with the world has changed as a result of that.

Live loved

I am beginning to experience what it means to live loved. It changes everything. Life takes on a whole new perspective: I do not feel obligated or bound by anything, I am free to be myself within the context of a loving relationship with my Father. God is love, and He wants me to experience that love and be free within it. Because of that, I can live a life filled with love and demonstrate that love to others. After all, "God so loved the world that He gave..." and Jesus told us to love one another just as He loved us. In order to do that, we must be able to receive love ourselves. How can we love, if we have not received His love? It would be superficial, limited to mere physical or emotional affection. But God desires to take us deeper into a love that surpasses that between friends, romantic partners or spouses, into *agape* love, unconditional and selfless love. To love in such a way, we must first receive it ourselves. That is why God wants us to receive and experience His love.

The Word

In the beginning was the Word, and the Word was with God, and the Word was God (John 1:1).

This Word, Jesus, came to reveal love to us. In His earthly life He fully expressed the image of the Father. He even said, "If you have seen Me, you have seen the Father." So, what do we think God is like? Do we see Him as being like Jesus? Or as a different, distant figure from the Old Testament? It can be confusing to have a divided perception of God, as if He were somehow two-faced, so that we could never be sure which face we would encounter. My view of God used to be more aligned with an old covenant perspective; but Jesus was awesome so I focused mostly on Him. But there is no difference between the Father, the Son, and the Holy Spirit in their nature of love. They are all expressions of love, and they want us to experience that love.

The Word spoken of here encompasses us, because we were spoken into existence based on the thoughts and desires of God's heart. When we connect deeply with God's heart, we are just like a baby in the womb. I do not remember being in the womb, although I have had to deal with some issues related to it. But if I could remember, I would have been surrounded by amniotic fluid, feeling my mother's heartbeat and receiving nourishment through the umbilical cord. It would have been a warm, safe, and secure place. Figuratively speaking, that is exactly where God wants to bring us back to – a place of safety and security in which we feel the Father's heartbeat.

When we had our first two children, we were not aware of how important it is to speak truth, bless, and empower your children while they are still in the womb. However, with our third and fourth children we had gained new revelation and began speaking truth, blessing, and empowering them even before they were born. In a similar way, God wants us to be able to hear His thoughts, His words, and feel His heartbeat and the rhythm of love so that we can experience His fullness.

Look at that scripture in the Mirror Bible translation:

To go back to the very beginning is to find the Word already present there; face to face with God. The Word is I am; God's eloquence echoes and concludes in him. The Word equals God (John 1:1 Mirror).

The Word is God's expression, His echo, and it reveals who we are. Without God, our image of ourselves will come from external sources. But when we engage in a deep relationship with Him, the image He reflects back to us is who He created us to be, not the distorted image we might have of ourselves based on the world's perception. God wants to restore us to an intimacy of relationship in His presence.

Refreshing

Therefore repent and return, so that your sins may be wiped away, in order that times of refreshing may come from the presence of the Lord (Acts 3:19).

That word 'repent' (from *metanoia*, meaning 'with mind') really does not mean feeling sorry for something: it is about radically shifting our thinking to align with God's mind. When God speaks, we repent by agreeing with Him. It is a shift from what we think about ourselves to embracing what He thinks about us. That is not easy if we cannot hear His thoughts about us. Without hearing from God, our information comes from what others have said about us or what we believe about ourselves, all of it influenced by nature, nurture, or trauma.

God wants to deal with all that and enable us to hear His voice directly, revealing who we truly are. We can return to that place of intimacy where His mind is revealed – the place we came from, where we were birthed out of His desire. And that is where the sin, which speaks of our lost identity, can be wiped away. In Greek, it reads *hymeis ho hamartia*, that is, 'our the sin', which does not make sense in English; so we have lost the word 'the' in our English Bibles, obscuring the fact that it is specific, and in the singular. What Adam led us into was our fallen image, because the word *hamartia* (sin) means 'without image'. 'Sin' is a loss of identity, not something we do. The behaviours we call 'sins' arise from that loss of identity, mostly from trying to get it back by seeking after it in all the wrong places.

God wants to wipe away our lost identity and bring times of refreshing through His presence. 'Refreshing' in that verse is *anapsyksis* in Greek. It is much more than a cool drink or a breeze on a summer day: it means breathing easily again, being revived, experiencing cool fresh air and finding true refreshment. It is about renewal, restoration, and the recovery of the breath of life that comes from being in God's presence. His presence is always with us and in us, as we are in Him. So those 'times of refreshing' are the renewal and restoration that comes from God's presence. That is why intimacy is so important.

Then the Lord God formed man of dust from the ground, and breathed into his nostrils the breath of life; and man became a living being (Genesis 2:7).

Our very life comes from the breath of God, and He wants to refresh us with His presence and breathe life back into us. God breathes into us, we breathe out. And then we breathe in the breath of God again, and so on. The rhythm of life is closely associated with YHWH, the name of God – I recall watching a 'Nooma' video by Rob Bell[2] years ago, where he pointed out that Yod, Hei, Vav, Hei actually sounds like breathing, and we use it that way in some of our activations.

Just as Jesus breathed on His disciples and imparted the Holy Spirit to them, so too He wants to refresh us, breathing His life back into us again. All are made alive in Christ through His resurrection, and He wants to restore relationship, identity, and intention for our lives. He wants us to look into His face, have Him breathe into us, and be restored to our original condition – a restored walking relationship with the Father's presence. That is truly refreshing.

---

[2] Available by subscription at https://watch.studygateway.com/nooma/videos/nooma-breathe-014

But it is not just about going back to what Adam was; rather it is about becoming what Adam would have become. He was sinless, but he was not yet perfected as a son. There is more to be restored in our relationship than just being alive. We are meant to become the fullness of a living being, a spirit being like God, because we are made as sons of God in His image.

I came across a quote that really struck me. It said, "Jesus is not the window showing us whom we can become. He is a mirror showing us who we already are." Religion often focuses on what we might become one day, in the future, maybe 'after we die and go to heaven'. But when we look into the face of God, we see our true identity from His perspective; when we realise who we already are, that realisation empowers us to live accordingly. We become like what we behold.

So what are we looking at? What is capturing our attention? That is what will shape and transform our lives. If we consider what we spend most of our time focusing on, it will give us a clue about what is happening in our lives. God desires a face-to-face encounter. He wants us to experience His love and truth in that deep embrace and connection.

Activation #2: Breathe

Now I encourage you to take a moment to do a short exercise where the Father wants to embrace you and breathe life into you. He wants to breathe His truth, His word into your being. He wants to breathe His love, acceptance, and purpose into your heart. So let's engage in this moment of encounter with Him.

To stream the audio, scan the QR code or visit the resources page.

Take a moment now to close your eyes and fix your thoughts on the Father. Do not just close your eyes and let your mind wander aimlessly or try to clear it completely, as in some forms of eastern meditation in which you might open yourself up to anything. In biblical meditation, we fix our thoughts on God, who is here with us, ready to breathe into us.

When we engage our imagination, we start thinking in a way that forms a picture in our mind, and then we can use that picture to connect and interact. What unfolds from there is not up to us, but we can activate and experience it.

> So I would encourage you,
> close your eyes and start thinking about the Father,
> face to face with you.
>
> He wants to give you a hug.
> He wants to embrace you.
> He wants to be heart to heart with you.
> He wants the rhythm of His heart
> to bring your heart into an alignment
> and into rest and peace.
>
> As those thoughts form in your imagination,
> begin to receive that embrace, that hug,
> that heart-to-heart.
>
> Then allow Him to breathe the words of life into you,
> to breathe His life essence into your being;
> into your spirit,
> into your soul.
> As He does that,
> let the vast sum of His thoughts about you
> begin to impregnate you,
> begin to be incubated in you,
> to be planted in you,
> to be fruitful in you.

I encourage you to be open and engage with the Father in this way every day. When you wake up in the morning, allow yourself to be embraced by the Father, heart to heart. We can embrace people on our right hand without being heart to heart, but when we embrace on the left side, it becomes heart to heart. God always embraces us heart-to-heart.

As we engage with the Father and He reveals things to us, we can meditate and ask Him to reveal anything about our own parental journey, our own father journey. Reflect on that and allow God to speak to you. We do not spend enough time reflecting, perhaps because we prefer not to go there, or we may be too busy to take the time out. But if we desire intimacy with the Father, it is good to reflect on the father issues in our own life. Ask the Father to reveal any areas that could be a problem for you. Reflect on your own childhood and ask Him to show you how He sees it.

It is important to examine how that experience has affected us and whether we are still influenced by it. Sometimes there may be blind spots where we do not realise the impact it has had on us until those things are uncovered. I believe God will begin to uncover them, not just for the sake of it but because He desires to meet with us and bring us into wholeness. He wants to bring healing and restoration, to restore His image in us and breathe words of life back into us.

Father

Looking back at my own childhood, I mostly remember the good experiences, as we often tend to do. We push away bad memories, especially if they were extremely traumatic or we carry anger towards them. In my own childhood, I had a great time, mostly doing my own thing with my friends. I did not have a particularly great time with my Dad, but I still enjoyed myself. However, I did sense that there was something missing – fatherly affirmation. So my affirmation came from my friends and eventually from others, mostly girls.

I learned that my father came from a broken home. His own father had left him when he was around 8 years old, so he never had a role model. I do not blame him for that, and I understand that is why it was hard for him to provide me with one. It was not his fault per se, but he still had choices, and perhaps he could have learned to be a better father. However, people rarely talked about such matters in those days.

I know that he felt rejected, and he was always searching for something in his life that would make him feel accepted. He carried the weight of being abandoned by his father, and perhaps he made judgments about that which affected him, as unforgiveness usually does. From my own experience, I had to deal with generational issues and familiar spirits related to those needs and the emotional pain that stemmed from them. The emotional pain I felt was mostly not caused directly by my Dad, but by the substitutes for him that I turned to. We all experience hurt, relational damage and pain from different sources.

So my father started with a disadvantage, and as a result, I began life with emotional and spiritual disadvantages because he was not emotionally or spiritually present for me. He was not able to show me that he loved me, and he never once said those words to me. There was no physical affection either. I was affected by the lack of those things – any damage was caused by what he did not do rather than what he did. There was no physical or verbal violence; in fact, there was no verbal communication at all. I never had a real conversation with him in my entire life, which might sound strange, but that was my reality. It is no surprise that I struggled with communication when I was growing up.

He never came to watch me play sports or support me in anything I did, despite my involvement in various teams. That was normal to me. But when other children's fathers showed up, something inside would register that there was something amiss, even though I might explain it away. I went to a school ten miles from my home, I could justify him not coming, but deep down it still had an impact. So there was no obvious abuse, only emotional abuse, which hits just as hard, maybe even harder. It messes you up. I did not have the love or emotional support of a father, however much I longed for it, so I started seeking comfort from others.

Relying on those substitute relationships caused all kinds of pain. By selfishly trying to fulfil my needs through others, I ended up hurting myself and them. No one can fully replace your real father. I did have a really awesome uncle who took me to church and spent time with me, and he was great. For the first four or five years of my life, I mostly looked to my uncle as a father figure, and I even have pictures of him doing things with me that my own father never did. But then he had his own children, and I felt rejected all over again. Over the years, although God met me in various encounters to help me deal with all of this, I could never really think of God as a father. It did not even cross my mind. I would talk to Jesus, or to 'the Lord', depending on the kind of prayer I was praying, but I never talked to the Father. Ever.

The first time I connected with God as Father was in 1989. It was a few years after I had been baptised in the spirit, and I was becoming more attuned to spiritual things. I was in a small group of people worshipping, when I felt God saying to me, 'I am your Father.' I could actually feel His arms around me. It was so real that I melted. Tears were streaming down my face. People around me were wondering what was happening, but I could not begin to explain it because I was overwhelmed with emotion. It was also the first time I ever saw an angel. It was a powerful experience, and it marked the beginning of my journey into a relationship with the Father.

It took time, because I was still struggling with the whole concept. But I felt His presence, His arms around me, and after a while I started to talk to Him through the Bible and prayer, which was mostly a one-way conversation. I did most of the talking, and I could not hear Him saying anything to me. But significantly, I was talking to Him as Father, which was a real change in my thinking.

You see, whilst the root issue was my father wounds, it showed up as rejection, which is common. I was already wounded, so when I experienced rejection and hurt from other people, it just made everything worse. Eventually, though, once I became part of a group that focused on ministry and healing, things began to change.

In the Methodist Church and the Brethren, we did not really have personal prayer ministry. People might pray for you, or they might not. But when I got baptised in the spirit and we started a church, it became a priority. There was a great deal of ministry happening. The environment was such that it brought everything to the surface, sometimes in the most unexpected ways. I can still remember some of those moments vividly. The two main issues that surfaced in me were betrayal and rejection. I realised there was a lot of betrayal in my life. And even after that, until I discovered the reason why I was open to betrayal, it was as if I had a sign on my forehead saying, 'Betray me.' I had people close to me betray me in various ways, so there was a lot of brokenness.

Then as we dug deeper, many hidden emotions started to surface, emotions that I had buried or did not even know were there, and mostly negative. You see, when I first got hurt, I made a vow to myself that I would never allow myself to be hurt like that again. I remember it so clearly. I was on a bus on my way home, and my first long-term girlfriend of six months had told me she wanted to take the summer off. I was devastated. I even manipulated her into changing her mind by crying for five hours straight. I know, it sounds crazy now. But on that bus ride, I made a vow. I said, "I will not be hurt like that again." That vow shut down my emotions completely.

From that point on, I appeared thick-skinned, unemotional and seemingly immune to hurt. But, of course, I did get hurt, it was just that it did not show on the surface. Deep inside I carried wounds, hurts, and pains that I never expressed but were festering within. When I started receiving ministry to help deal with my emotions, the people praying for me described it as like praying for a block of granite. That is how emotionally hardened I had become. I had built a protective layer around my heart, determined not to be hurt or betrayed again. When my emotions began to open up, I felt incredibly vulnerable. It seemed like everyone was constantly attacking me. Those closest to me had been waiting for my emotions to open up for years, and when they finally did, I became defensive and angry. But for them it was better to see some emotions rather than none at all.

Eventually the sources of those emotions surfaced, revealing the deeper issues, including my father wounds. I had never realised that they were at the root of it all. I only saw where I had been hurt, never suspecting that it stemmed from my unmet need for a father's love. I had closed it all off. It was through my own children that God worked on me. And once it opened up, thankfully, God stepped in as Father and began to heal those wounds. He spoke to me, and I started to learn how to address my own situation. I had to confront it and go through the process of forgiving my Dad, releasing him from the debt he owed me that burdened my life. I knew it was the right thing to do, so I did it. I did not feel any strong emotions. I did not cry or feel overwhelmed, but I made the choice to forgive because I did not want to carry that burden anymore.

Our relationship had always been practically non-existent. We had a lot of teaching in the church about forgiving and releasing, and I found that it worked. I felt liberated, to the point where I went to see him, telling him I forgave him and that I loved him. I even gave him a hug. He stood there like a tree, unsure of how to respond because he was broken and wounded himself.

Then, something happened that shattered my illusions. I saw a picture in my mind of myself sitting on my Dad's knee, wearing a little red bow tie and blue shorts. This was an image I recognised: it was from a black and white photograph, and I remembered it vividly because we used to have it at home. But the picture was a complete sham. It was just a pose for the photograph, something that never happened in real life. And as soon as that revelation hit me, a wave of emotions flooded over me like an avalanche. It was as if everything about my childhood and everything else just came crashing down, and I felt completely exposed and raw. But it also enabled me to choose to confront it and deal with it. Again I faced it head-on and chose to forgive him. Much later, shortly before he died, I took my own children to visit him; but due to his brokenness he was still unable to receive our love.

Then, in 1994, I was about to move to Barnstaple to start a church and was travelling up from Cornwall once a week for teaching and foundational work. During a meeting with a group of people, we were worshipping, and I was about to speak. Suddenly, it felt as if I was observing myself on the floor, wailing and sobbing uncontrollably. All my pain and anguish were being released, and I cried for a solid 40 minutes.

The people who were there expecting me to teach did not know what to do with me as they witnessed this emotional outpouring. Fortunately, they did nothing, which was exactly the right course of action. It was simply a release of all the emotional pain that had built up inside me. Once it came to an end, I stood up and it seemed as if I had shed a hundred tons of weight. I felt incredibly light because I was no longer carrying the burden of all that emotional baggage. It was a liberating experience, and paved the way so that two years later, I could have my first encounter with the Father in heaven.

That happened during a Sunday morning worship session in a school. We had an incredibly talented saxophonist, Mike Collins, who played a soaring note on his saxophone; and as I closed my eyes, I felt myself being lifted into heaven. I was completely unaware of my surroundings as the Father placed me on His knee. In that moment, He restored everything my earthly father had never provided for me. It was a genuine father-son relationship, in which He played with me, cared for me and healed me: I finally knew that I had a real Father who loved me deeply. This was the opposite of what I had experienced with my earthly father, and I found it truly extraordinary.

Over the years, my relationship with the Father has continued to develop. I began to engage and have real conversations with Him. I felt healed and restored to a degree where I believed there was nothing more to address. Father issues and past hurts lead us to protect ourselves, and I now understand that I was trying to safeguard myself from further pain.

God showed me that the strategies we use to keep ourselves safe can easily become prisons we have created for ourselves. Those who struggle with rejection often respond in two ways: either they become difficult and prickly, never allowing anyone to get too close, always striking first to keep people away; or they become compliant, never wanting to upset anyone and avoiding rejection at all costs. These are the kinds of issues God wants to address in our lives.

In 2010, I attended a conference where God spoke to me about giving Him my full attention. On the way there, I received a clear message from Him that He wanted me to be fully present with Him, rather than focused on the teachings and activities. So, although it felt strange to isolate myself and not engage with others, I decided to be with God alone. As the worship began, my heart experienced a level of intimacy I had never thought possible. The depth of love I felt from God was incredible, and it transformed my heart. I yearned for more of that intimacy – it was like a hunger inside me. The unfamiliar songs, mostly those of Jesus Culture and Misty Edwards, all spoke of that intimacy; and for the first time I actually experienced it. On the way back home, God instructed me to embark on a 40-day fast.

During the two years leading up to this, I had been yearning to return to heaven. In 2008, I had my initial encounter, and now, after this recent experience, I wanted it even more. Then, I received a prophetic word in a letter from a friend. It mentioned that God had seen my heart, and knew exactly what was in it – my desire to return to the intimacy of heaven. The letter even said, 'Ascend to where I am,' and I was thrilled, thinking, 'Yippee, I'm going back to heaven!'

So I embarked on the 40-day fast. Initially I went through a gruelling 19 days of trying everything in my power, struggling and striving to ascend into heaven. I 'repented' for everything I could think of (I still held to the traditional understanding of repentance, which was saying sorry), especially for anything that might have hindered my access to heaven. I endured 19 days of intense fire. My body felt like it was burning, even my bones. Eventually I reached a point of surrender. I said, "Okay, I give up. If You want this to happen, You have to do it."

Then, finally, I entered heaven. I spent two incredible weeks there, engaging with Jesus and the Holy Spirit, and receiving some astounding revelations. However, I had still not yet encountered the Father there; and that fact lingered in the back of my mind. One day, Jesus approached me and said, "You have a father wound." I argued with Him – not the smartest move, because you do not win arguments with Jesus. I believed I had dealt with everything regarding my Dad, so I insisted that I did not have a father wound. But Jesus looked into my heart and showed me significant scar tissue that remained even though the wound had healed. He asked, "Do you want the Father to heal your wound?" And I responded "Oh, yes!" In that moment, the Father came and gazed into my eyes, saying just one thing: "I love you. I love you. I love you. I love you." He repeated those words for what felt like an eternity (it was 45 minutes in earthly time), removing all the scar tissue from my heart. That was an intense experience.

Although I had received healing and restoration from my wounds, I still carried the residue of the scars; and that had hindered my relationship with Him. The inner healing and all the ministry I had gone through had only brought me from a negative place to zero. Being fathered was a key element I had been missing. As the Father spoke those words of love, each one healed my heart, causing the scar to vanish. Then He opened up realms of experience that surpassed my wildest imagination. He took me into places of deep intimacy, including the garden of my heart, which I had never known before. He began to father me, and it was a revelation. All earthly figures of authority had let me down, used me or had their own agendas. But the Father had no agenda other than blessing me and bringing me into full sonship. This is what He desires for all of us.

All my experiences led me back to where the Father wanted to father me. He continued to do just that, taking me through experiences that challenged my preconceived notions of who He was. The distant God, the angry God, the disciplinarian God – I had to confront and let go of all those false ideas.

Trust became the key: learning to trust the Father opened up a whole new world. One day, He asked me, "How do I make you feel? How do you know I love you?" By that point, we had engaged in numerous conversations, and I hesitated to answer quickly because I always seemed to get it wrong. But as I pondered, I realised that intimacy, for me, was not about warm and fuzzy feelings in being embraced by God, as others often described. I had experienced incredible encounters, but that was not the essence of it for me either. When the Father asked how I felt His love, I realised it was simply being with Him, spending quality time in His presence. That was my language of love towards God. If I had been searching for the warm fuzzy feelings, I would have missed the depth of what I was experiencing.

If you have ever read about love languages in marriage, you will know that we often mistakenly assume that our spouse has the same love language we do. We then try to express love towards the other based on how we want to be loved ourselves, rather than understanding what it takes for them to feel loved. It can be the same with God. For me, it involves spending a lot of time in conversation with Him, sitting in green pastures or in a garden. For you it may be entirely different. We may have a distorted perception of His love, but when we get intimate with Him, we can begin to understand how He loves and fathers us.

To bring this testimony to a conclusion, let me tell you about an experience I had during a conference in Arizona in 2016. I was leading a session on experiencing the Father's love. When I lead activations, I try not to get too immersed myself because I can easily get lost in it (as has happened several times, especially online). This time, I could not resist being drawn into the experience. Suddenly, I found myself in the Court of the Upright in heaven, and the Father led me to meet my earthly father. I had not even realised that he was in heaven – he had never openly professed any faith during his time on earth, unlike my mother. But there he was, walking up to me just like in the movie *The Shack*. He embraced me tightly and told me he was proud of me, something he had never done in his life. Of course, I was overwhelmed with tears, trying to compose myself for the next part of the teaching I had to do.

But eventually I gave up because the floodgates had opened. It was a kiss from God, bringing closure to that entire situation. Even though God the Father had repeatedly told me how much He loved me and how proud He was of me, to have my earthly father affirm me in that way meant the world to me. It opened up new levels of the depth of the Father's love, understanding how much He loves me, how much He loves the entire creation, and how love is at the core of His being. This whole journey took me deeper and deeper into that understanding. Now I enjoy an ongoing daily conversational relationship with God. I walk with Him, engaging in discussion, sitting down and talking with Him.

I desired to experience His love not only in heaven, but within myself as well, so I opened up my first love gate in the spirit, engaging with God in the garden of my heart, embracing His presence within me. That is as real as any other spiritual or physical dimension. Like the TARDIS in *Doctor Who*, it is bigger on the inside than on the outside. Within me, there is a relative dimension in space where my spirit and soul reside, made of spiritual material, and I consciously engage with them. I love spending time within myself engaging with God, because He dwells within me. It helps ground me and make it real. It is a realm within my soul, within my heart, where I have learned to connect with Him, and where He affirms, reveals and unveils the truth of my identity as a beloved son. He desires the same for all of us. We can all engage within ourselves and in the heavenly realms.

Worth and purpose

I love going to the Throne of Grace and to the Father's garden – those are key places of intimacy for me. On my first visit to the Throne of Grace, I was not expecting what happened there: I thought I would just receive some grace. But instead, the Father picked me up, placed me on His lap, and held me close to His heart. I could feel the rhythm of His heartbeat, and it was so comforting that I fell asleep. And while I rested, He was at work, taking care of everything I had unloaded onto Him. I didn't have to do it all by myself.

We can all have experiences like that, where we surrender our burdens to Him and let Him handle it all, because we have all been adopted into God's family. We all have a new name now: not slaves or stewards, not servants, but sons. And because of that, we have a new legal standing. We are righteous. We are fully accepted. We are not alienated or condemned, except in our own thinking. You see, "as a man thinks in his heart, so is he" (see Proverbs 23:7 NKJV). However you see yourself, your actions will tend to align with it.

God wants us to see ourselves as we truly are; to give us experiences that will change our thinking and align it with His truth. We have this new family relationship and access to God's presence in heaven. We have a new image – the image of Jesus – and we are being restored into that image. However, the enemy wants to rob us of that. If he can hinder our understanding of being sons, it will also hinder our relationship with the Father. We will never fully become who God intends us to be if we keep striving to be something that He has already made us to be. That's why He wants to reveal our sonship to us, in a father-child relationship with Him.

The question is, will we let Him do it? And that comes down to whether we trust Him. I thought I trusted Him until He showed me that I did not. There were still areas in my soul where I sought control and tried to gain my identity from what I did, seeking His approval. The truth is, we are already approved of and He wants to reveal and unveil that truth to us. We may need to forgive and release our own parents, especially our fathers, if they failed to truly demonstrate who God is as a Father. We might not even be angry or bothered by it, but if we do not address it, it can become a stumbling block and hinder us.

So, if your parents were imperfect, if they did not provide everything you needed to nurture you into who you were created to be; if they burdened you or controlled you; if they did not show unconditional love or disciplined you harshly, take some time to reflect on that. Do a little inventory.

We need a process of restoration, and only God can restore us. We can meet God as our Father. We can have encounters with Him, and He wants to meet us in that way. But let's go beyond just seeing it as an exercise. In the next chapter, we will do an activation and focus on healing and restoration using communion. I encourage you to think about it ahead of time and give God the opportunity to show you if there are any areas that need resolution. Are there any unmet needs within you? Are you still seeking affirmation from others because you have not fully received it from the Father? We will run into trouble if we keep seeking approval from others because they will inevitably let us down. Nobody is perfect. And then we might feel betrayed, wounded, and hurt, causing us to build walls around us.

There were times when I could be surrounded by people, even in a small group, and still feel alone; I would have my barriers up, protecting myself from getting hurt. Despite being in the presence of others, I felt isolated. But when those barriers finally came down and my wounds from my father and from betrayal were healed, suddenly I was free to be myself. I no longer had to compare myself to anyone else. I could embrace vulnerability, be open, and freely share.

Now I know that other people's opinions and judgments do not define me: it is what God says about me that matters. I know how deeply He loves me. I know the beautiful things He has spoken over my life and the revelations He has given me. That is how I measure my worth and purpose. So, let others say whatever they want, positive or negative, neither have any effect on me. I have learned to forgive and release people, especially when they are acting hurtfully. My identity and confidence come solely from God, my Heavenly Father, who has lovingly shaped me into who I am today.

Reflect

So here is what I urge you to do: allow God to uncover any unresolved areas in your life. Maybe there are still some lingering scars that need healing and restoration. God cares for you more than you care about yourself, more than anyone else could possibly care about you. He also wants to help you and to fulfil every need you have. He put those needs for acceptance, approval, affirmation, and significance in you because He wants to meet them. So if you are trying to find fulfilment for them from your spouse, friends, children, or anyone else, they will never be able to give you what God can give you. If you are seeking fulfilment elsewhere, you are looking in the wrong place. Let Him reveal who you truly are and show you where you came from. Let Him take you back to that wonderful place of security within His embrace, where you can truly shine and understand your purpose in life. But beware: do not rush into chasing your purpose without truly knowing who you are. Otherwise, you can easily fall into the trap of striving and trying to discover your purpose through endless activity.

These are deep questions we all face. Take some time to let these things sink in. Find somewhere quiet where you are or go for a walk if you prefer. Give yourself that space now to ask the important questions: is there anything still unresolved in my relationship with God as Father, or in my relationships with my earthly father or others?

If you cannot do that just now, please read no further until you have been able to do so. Then, in the next chapter, we will engage in restoration and healing, seeing God work in those areas as you surrender and hand them over to Him.

4. Healing Father Wounds

The previous chapter primarily involved exploring our relationship with our earthly father and our heavenly Father, delving deeper into that connection. We also addressed the need for healing in this area. If God has uncovered some of those things for us, then it is important to activate and engage with this aspect. In this chapter we will begin by looking to engage with God particularly around any father issues, and seeing Him open up His heart as a Father.

Training our senses

If you are unfamiliar with the idea of activation and engagement, and with spiritual experiences, you may be concerned that you are 'just making it up' or that it is 'all in your mind'. Please understand that all you experience, even in the physical world, happens in your mind. When you look at this book, it is actually your mind that develops an image of it, not your eyes. Your eyes merely capture light and convert it into electrical signals, which are then sent to your brain through the optic nerve. What is more, because of the way the lens in your eye captures light, your brain actually receives that image upside-down, but it has learned to interpret it correctly, and turn it the right way up.

Similarly with hearing, you perceive sound when your ears detect pressure waves and convert them into auditory signals that eventually reach your brain. Your brain has learned to interpret these signals. But if someone were to speak to you in a language you do not know, you would hear but not understand, since your brain has not been exposed to that language and its sounds.

We have learned to interpret various sounds in our environment, such as the sound of a bat on ball or an ambulance siren. We recognise these sounds because we have encountered them before, and our brain identifies them. We have developed the ability to interpret sounds and images in the physical world, but hardly any of us have been taught how to interpret our spiritual experiences.

Those spiritual experiences can also provide us with valuable information. Just as our eyes and ears transmit electrical impulses to the brain, our spirit sends signals too. However, they are not actually processed through our eyes or ears; so when we talk about hearing God's voice or seeing a vision, that is not physical hearing or physical seeing. So do not get too caught up in whether you can 'see' visually in the spirit, or 'hear' audibly. It is the fact of communication and the information and revelation we receive that are important, not the means by which we perceive it.

The book of Hebrews tells us that through practice, we can train our senses to discern spiritual matters. It is a skill we can learn and develop. We can become more attuned to the spiritual atmosphere around us, to pick up on what is happening in the angelic realm and even in other people.

Jesus perceived what people were thinking and feeling. It was not just about body language or facial expressions for Him: I believe He was actually able to tap into the electrical impulses they were giving off. Scientists have detected electrical signals emitted by our hearts, and they create an energy field far larger than that created by our brains. Our spirits too can detect that energy; they are constantly feeding us information but most of us do not know how to interpret it.

That is where practice and learning come in. In the *Engaging God* programme[3], we teach people how to practise hearing, seeing, perceiving and knowing. We all receive spiritual insights in different forms and expressions because we are all wired differently. Some describe it as hearing, some as seeing, and some as knowing or sensing. I started out by learning to hear God's voice in conversation. So when I am engaging with God, I would say that I not only see things but also hear His voice. And even when I am not seeing anything, I can still hear and stay aware of what is going on because I have learned how to know.

---

[3] Visit eg.freedomarc.org to find more information about this and get a free 2-week trial.

Living in dual realms

I am operating in dual realms of heaven and earth all the time, but I was not able to do that until my soul and spirit were separated and reintegrated. In the past, I was continually stepping, soul and spirit, into the spiritual realm and then back into the physical realm every day. Years ago, Ian Clayton shared with us his exercises in stepping in and out, and they were very helpful to get us started. But honestly, I prefer to stay in the spiritual realm. I do not want to keep stepping out. Now my soul steps out but my spirit stays in, and I have learned how to shift the focus of my soul's consciousness to be aware of what I am doing in heaven.

That did not happen overnight. Nobody laid hands on me so that suddenly I just had these abilities. I practised for years to develop my hearing, seeing, knowing, and living in the heavenly realms, so that now I can describe to someone what my spirit is doing in the realms of heaven even while I am talking to them here in this realm. Of course, I could just close my eyes and engage in the spiritual realm all the time, but that would not be very helpful for my daily life on earth or my role in teaching and mentoring others. Through practice I have learned to draw from that realm while actively engaging in this physical one.

I have also learned to perceive the spiritual atmosphere in a room, and to discern the presence of the angelic. It is like using spiritual sonar. I send out a 'ping' in the spirit, and I receive an echo back that tells me what is out there. It comes quite naturally to me now, and I do not even really have to think about it. But I do not do it all the time because it can be distracting to see everything going on around me. Have you heard about people having an aura? That is just another way of referring to what I am describing. It is an atmosphere around people, which may be positive or negative: joyful, peaceful, confused, fearful and so on. You can learn to pick that up. I reserve that for when it feels right or necessary, otherwise it could become just a party trick. I could not receive that ability from somebody else, and you too will need to discover it for yourself. It is all about practice and learning.

Relax

So, during these activations, I encourage you to relax and not push too hard to see things. When you strive too much, it becomes difficult to see clearly, or what you see might feel forced. Just allow yourself to breathe naturally and ease into it.

We are going to step into the realm of heaven. Jesus wants to engage with us, and the Father wants to embrace us. I usually start by engaging in my own spirit because that is an easier place to begin. God is within me. The scriptures tell us that He has come to dwell in us. Engage with that truth. You might wonder, "How do I engage in my own spirit?" The fact is, you are already within yourself. Your mind and soul are already there. You just have to make a conscious choice to engage with them. It is a matter of desire, choice and faith. You can say, "I am going to engage with this."

Behold, I stand at the door and knock; if anyone hears My voice and opens the door, I will come in to him and will dine with him, and he with Me (Revelation 3:20).

I often use that scripture as a gateway to this experience. "Behold, I stand at the door and knock." Which door is He standing at? Not the physical doors in the room, but the door within me where He resides. His kingdom is within, where He rules and reigns. There is a place in my spirit where He is, and it has a door that I have to open. He will not force it open. The verse says, "If anyone hears my voice..." which tells us that He is calling out as well as knocking, and I believe He is probably saying, "Open the door. Let me in!" (Or, "let me out," depending on how you look at it).

He is seeking relationship, because the verse continues, "I will come in and dine with him, and he with Me." Dining in that culture represented intimacy: John leaned on Jesus' breast as they reclined during meals. It was a time of connection, fellowship, relaxation, and friendship.

Some might say, "I don't know how to open the door." It is by choice. We close our eyes, visualise a door, and choose to open it. We welcome the presence of God to fill us, and we actively engage that presence. Then we ask the Father to guide us where He wants to take us.

Perhaps He wants to take us into the garden of our own heart, where green pastures and quiet waters await. There, He may bring healing to our father wounds or speak to us and share something. Or He can lead us through that door, which is like a wormhole to heaven, straight into Eden, the Father's garden.

The river of life (that we read about in Ezekiel 47) is flowing from heaven into us. For most people, it trickles under the door. Once we open the door, it begins at our ankles, rises to our knees, waist, and eventually floods all over us. Rivers of living water are flowing from our inmost being, just as Jesus promised. By choice, you can create an atmosphere where these rivers flow intentionally. The tiny trickle most people experience has produced the fruit and gifts of the Spirit to the extent it can. However, when we open that door, the river of life can flow abundantly, bringing life wherever it goes. That was its intended purpose from the beginning.

When you open the door, you can follow that river of life and engage the tree of life, the throne of grace, and the judgment seat. In a later chapter we will explore engaging the fire of God's presence at the judgment seat, as there may be aspects of our scrolls that require refinement and purification. There are many ways to approach this, but this time allow the Father to embrace you and take you either into your garden, or His. There you can lie down and rest, engage, and let Him heal you, speaking words of love to restore and make you whole.

Take a moment now to relax. It can be a struggle to truly relax as we tend to overthink or analyse. Find a comfortable position, perhaps rotate your shoulders and gently ease your head from side to side to release physical tension, and allow yourself to unwind mentally and emotionally.

HEALING

Activation #3 Healing Father Wounds

Now, imagine that Jesus is knocking on the door of your spirit.

To stream the audio, scan the QR code or visit the resources page.

Close your eyes
and picture this door
in your imagination.
It can be any door you choose,
but it represents the door within you.
Behind this door,
the Father is inviting you to open it
and let Him in.

Choose to open the door.
Picture yourself reaching out in the spirit,
opening the door,
and welcoming His presence to come and fill you;
welcoming His presence to embrace you,
as a father embraces his child.

As you sense His presence around you,
you may feel peace, love,
or even have a full visionary experience of His embrace.

In your thoughts, engage with His thoughts
so His thoughts will begin to operate in your thinking
as He speaks to you
as He embraces you.

And consciously choose to ask Him to lead you
to the place of restoration,
healing and wholeness for you.

That might be following the river of life
into the garden of your own heart
where there will be a place for you and Him
to just sit in green pastures.

Or it may be that He then leads you
back through that first love gate you have opened
into the realm of Eden

where there is the river of life
and you can walk by the river of life.

Be open for the Father to begin to lead you
and take you to the place of restoration and healing
where He can speak His words of love into your heart.

Sometimes, walking in the realms of heaven,
there is just an amazing sense of fragrance,
and joy, and peace, and glory in the atmosphere.

But the Father has a garden
and you can walk with Him into that garden
or walk with Him into your garden.

Wherever you go, just lie down and rest.
Just lie down and consciously let everything go.

Begin to enjoy that deep sense
of the peace of His presence.

Then, if you carry any father wounds, or any scars,
consciously choose to open yourself to Him
and reveal those things to Him.
And if you are not sure,
allow Him to reveal those things to you.

Hear the Father's words:

"I love you."

"I love you."

"I love you."

"I love you."

"I love you."

Just hear the healing words
that will remove those scars
that will heal those wounds
and let the Father affirm you.

You are His beloved child.
He is pleased with you.
His soul delights in you.
It is His good pleasure to bless you and empower you
and bring you into wholeness.

So if you have never had the Father's love
just let Him love on you.
In that place of peace
in that place of rest
allow His healing words to envelop you
allow His love, joy and peace
to flood all around you.
You are safe and secure.

There are other places in the garden.
There are pools, there are waterfalls.
There are beautiful places.
Be open for whatever the Father wants to show you
whatever the Father wants to reveal to you
whatever the Father wants to impart to your spirit
let your spirit receive it.

So any barriers, any walls
any coping mechanisms,
any defence mechanisms
that you have developed to keep yourself safe
just surrender
and allow those walls and barriers to come down.
You are safe.

This is just an introduction into the fullness of what God wants to do. As you go to sleep tonight, return to that place of intimacy and engage your soul there. All night, the Father can be continuing His work in you, bringing you into wholeness, affirming you, restoring you, bringing you into sonship and healing any wounds, removing barriers and obstacles. He wants to take us into a place where our hearts are engaging with His presence in a way which begins to transform and change us and make us whole.

5. Communion

From the inside out

One of the most powerful experiences I have engaged with in seeing my life transformed is allowing the life of God, the presence of God, to purify me from the inside out. In the past, all the ministry I had received was from the outside in, trying to uncover underlying issues by peeling back successive layers. However, I came to realise that by working from the inside out, I could address these issues directly.

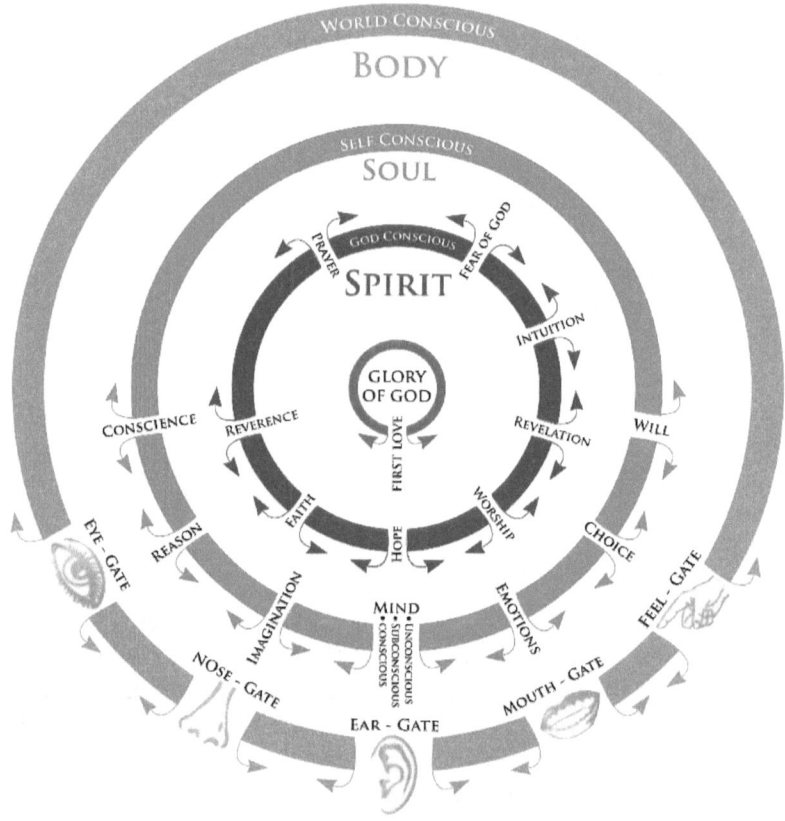

This 'gateways' diagram was first introduced to us by Ian Clayton in 2011, but versions of it have circulated for a century or more. God is within us, and He wants to fill us and flow from our innermost being, through the gateways of our spirit, soul, and body. God's presence resides in our spirit, which has its own senses or gateways that activate when His Spirit interacts with ours. Our soul also has gateways that primarily receive external information from the world around us. Our body connects us to the physical realm through the five physical senses: smell, taste, touch, sight, and hearing.

When I first began this journey, I was not even aware of these gateways, so I invited Jesus to walk through them in my spirit and show them to me. He exposed everything that did not belong there, including familiar spirits blocking, hindering and obstructing the flow. With His help my gateways were unblocked, and the river of life began to flow out from my spirit to my soul bringing healing and wholeness.

Our spirit is where we become God-conscious, intimately aware of God's presence. In our soul we are self-conscious; but we can cultivate a self-consciousness based on insights from our spirit rather than relying solely on external sources. It is also possible to become attuned to the world around us by seeing through the lens of our spirit, rather than through our physical senses alone. In this way, our physical senses such as touch and taste can be enriched or tempered by our spirit's perspective, which extends beyond the confines of the physical realm. Living this way, through our spirit, requires effort and intentional work.

But he who is joined to the Lord is one spirit with Him. (1 Corinthians 6:17 NKJV).

God desires us to be so intimately connected that we operate as one, and no one can really tell whether it is His Spirit or ours.

Now may the God of peace himself make you entirely holy, and may your whole spirit and soul and body be kept blameless in the presence of our Lord Jesus Christ. (1 Thessalonians 5:23 MLT).

Unlike the Modern Literal Translation quoted here, most of our English Bible versions prefer 'coming' in that verse to 'presence'. The Greek word is *parousia*, meaning 'presence'.

If it is translated 'coming', then it can only be fulfilled when Jesus comes, usually assumed to be sometime in the future. But Jesus is always coming; His presence is always with us; and this verse is describing a continual development rather than a future event. Our spirit, soul and body can be made whole, made complete, brought progressively into oneness, and it can be happening here and now.

God has shown me a means by which trauma can be turned into transformation[4]: it involves reflecting on our thoughts, feelings and sensations in response to present and past events. When we invite God to address the underlying causes, He frees us from their effects. We identify the areas within our subconscious which Jesus referred to as hard, stony, or weedy ground, where cares, anxieties, troubles, memories, hurts and pains have taken root. These areas influence our mindsets and behaviours and are often reinforced by familiar spirits that whisper and affirm negative patterns.

Communion can play a significant role in dealing with these issues. The body and blood of Jesus carry healing power and the capacity to make us whole.

Search me, O God, and know my heart;
Try me and know my anxious thoughts;
And see if there be any hurtful way in me,
And lead me in the everlasting way (Psalm 139:23-24).

David prays, "Search me, O God, and know my heart." That is what I did, as I allowed the Lord to walk with me in the depths of my heart, revealing its workings, and especially how memories affected different aspects of my life. He showed me the condition of my conscience, which was designed to direct and protect me. It was hardened and seared in some areas, failing to warn me of potentially dangers which I could have avoided. Throughout this searching and revealing, I spent significant time with Him, allowing Him to unveil and expose areas of my soul which He wanted to deal with. As David

---

[4] See *My Journey Beyond Beyond*, pp126-127.

wrote, God desires to lead us in the everlasting way, which is how we were formed in eternity.

Where it says, 'try me', that word relates to testing a substance to see if it is pure: it means 'to use a touchstone.' Is this pure gold? Is this pure silver? So God's presence tests our hearts and shows us the really good, healthy areas, as well as areas which are suffering from hurt or pain. God wants to transform our hearts to prepare us for our destiny. Communion is not just some religious ritual; it is a profound encounter with the very life and nature of God that He wants to impart to us.

Growing up, initially in the Methodist Church, I was not even permitted to take part in it. It made me wonder why others were allowed to whilst I could not. Even when I was older, it held little meaning or life-transforming power for me. Later, in the Brethren Church, it seemed like a funeral service: we remembered Jesus' death every Sunday, and that we were responsible for His suffering on the cross. Sometimes I felt emotional, but most of the time, I just felt guilty, focusing on my role as a terrible sinner who caused Jesus' to die. Any presentation of life was entirely lacking in those experiences.

As years went by, I came to realise it held much more depth and significance than I had previously thought. It has various names in different Christian traditions: Mass, communion, breaking bread, Eucharist, the sacrament, or the Lord's Supper. Regardless of the terminology used, the essence remains the same: we are applying the body and blood of Jesus to our lives, receiving His life-transforming power – or at least, we can be. I still found it hard to find a way of taking communion – and especially of leading it in a church setting – without it becoming repetitive or empty ritual. However, as I began to personally and intimately engage with God, communion began to take on a whole new revelation and dimension of truth and power.

The Roman Catholic concept of transubstantiation, which holds that the physical elements actually transform into the real physical body and blood of Jesus, is not accurate – it remains bread and wine, or whatever we use. However, when we take it in faith, it does carry power, because it holds the intention of God to transform and bring us into wholeness as we share in His life, body, and the power of His blood. It is not a physical transformation but a spiritual one. We can take communion at any time, eating and drinking of what symbolically represents His body and blood. When we do, it contains the life that God wants to impart to us at that time.

And when He had taken some bread and given thanks, He broke it and gave it to them, saying, "This is My body which is given for you; do this in remembrance of Me." (Luke 22:19).

"It is the Spirit who gives life; the flesh profits nothing; the words that I have spoken to you are spirit and are life." (John 6:63).

When Jesus instructed the Twelve to do this in remembrance of Him, He was not referring to the fact of His crucifixion alone. It is the wider aspect of the finished work of the cross that He wants us to embrace, as it all carries life. So the more we eat and drink this spiritually, the more life it will bring. Whenever you eat anything, you can consider it to represent the body and blood of Jesus. I affirm that I am receiving the life of God, not just physical nourishment and energy.

They were continually devoting themselves to the apostles' teaching and to fellowship, to the breaking of bread and to prayer (Acts 2:42).

In the early church they were continually devoted to breaking bread. They understood the power it contained and practised it daily, during their shared meals, which were an opportunity to fellowship with each other and with God. I encourage you to adopt a mindset where every time you eat, you see it as an opportunity for life to be imparted to you, rather than just consuming food for your body. It is your intention and your engagement that activates the power in it. Learning to apply the body and blood of Jesus through communion can be a significant factor in our transformation. It certainly was for me, once it went beyond being a religious practice to become a way of applying life continually.

You do not need to be limited to physical actions. You can step into heaven and embrace the power available there, allowing it to touch your soul. You can spiritually engage with it and enter the heavenly tabernacle where the table and the showbread symbolise the bread of life. You can take communion on the dance floor of your heart or in green pastures with God. In Psalm 23 God prepares a table before us: in the midst of the challenges and enemies in my life seeking to rob, kill, and destroy, I can choose to embrace life through communion and it will empower and transform me.

So it is not solely about physically eating and drinking; it is about activating our connection and engagement with God. When I first started using communion for transformation, I would go into the dance floor of my heart, where He revealed things I had never seen before. I had flashbacks to memories and experiences that had influenced my DNA for generations, and some were most unpleasant. I was deeply shocked when I began to see those negative aspects of my genetic past unveiled: it was like a process of death, exposing within me all that hindered my wholeness. But God exposed it so that He could heal and transform me.

I started recognising opportunities for communion in various contexts. One time I was engaging in Isaiah 6, "Woe is me! I am unravelled! Because I am a man of unclean lips, and I live amongst a people of unclean lips!" I saw it as a perfect moment to engage in communion, to have those hindrances unveiled, to be touched by the coals brought by the seraphim and experience the life and fire of God's presence. When the angel touched Isaiah's lips, it represented the cleansing of his lips, his heart and every aspect of his being. It can remove anything that prevents us from thinking of ourselves the way God does. It goes beyond 'sin' in the sense of bad behaviour; it encompasses everything that does not align with God's best for us, including false beliefs and thoughts. We can receive forgiveness, healing, and wholeness.

As we take communion beyond the veil, stepping into the heavenly realms, we are transformed and transfigured; we radiate light. We allow the process of refining and purifying to unfold even in areas of our lives hidden from us. Having our genetic makeup restored affects not only our spiritual but our physical, emotional and mental well-being as we open ourselves to Jesus, the living Word, who knows us intimately, loves us, and desires only the best for us.

Communion addresses at least three levels of transformation: behaviours that do not align with godliness, the motivations underlying those behaviours, and genetic factors and triggers. Through it we find redemption, forgiveness and restoration. It brings us out of the prison of sin and death into the realm of life. We are brought near to God by the blood of Jesus, cleansed and sanctified through communion:

... how much more will the blood of Christ, who through the eternal Spirit offered Himself without blemish to God, cleanse your conscience from dead works to serve the living God? (Hebrews 9:14).

Therefore Jesus also, that He might sanctify the people through His own blood, suffered outside the gate (Hebrews 13:12)

... and through Him to reconcile all things to Himself, having made peace through the blood of His cross; through Him, I say, whether things on earth or things in heaven (Colossians 1:20).

He will set us apart and work the transformation in our lives, as we turn over to Him any anxiety, worry, or whatever is not at peace in our life. By applying communion, we can enter into a place of peace.

I was a spiritual being before ever I was a physical one. But my ancestors also had a history, so when I became a physical being, it carried with it an inheritance mingled with different genetic seed. God showed me that I had particular genetic encoded material sequences which were not human. Before and after the flood there was a mingling of genetic material through overshadowing by fallen beings, long before modern GM techniques, and some was now present in my DNA. I tried everything I knew to overcome the resultant conduct in my life. I even got deliverance, but although things might improve for a few months, soon I would see those behaviours resurface in me.

It was not until I started to apply communion to those issues that I received revelation about specific genetic encoded material and sequences that had been altered in past generations. Trying to exert my willpower alone was a futile effort: it was a waste of energy to try to rule over something that should not even be there. Engaging with communion and allowing its power to restore and refine would be a far more effective approach. As I began to apply these revelations, God uncovered deep-rooted issues related to idolatry and other factors. His DNA holds the record of my identity as a son; so by engaging with His DNA through communion, I was able to address and finally resolve this generational genetic mixture.

In Hebrews it says that Melchizedek had no genealogy; since we are part of the order of Melchizedek, our genealogy need not have power over us. That does not just automatically occur when we encounter Jesus and recognise Him at work in us. Whilst He has done everything necessary for us to live in wholeness, we need to actively participate in the process and cooperate with Him to see that level of transformation.

Eat and not die

Through communion, death has no hold over me. The wages of sin is death, and Jesus has already dealt with sin. But if there are still remnants of death within me, inherited through my generational lines and encoded in my DNA, they are still able to manifest. I embrace the truth that Jesus is the living bread that came from heaven; by eating that bread, I will not die.

I am the bread of life. Your fathers ate the manna in the wilderness, and they died. This is the bread which comes down out of heaven, so that one may eat of it and not die. I am the living bread that came down out of heaven; if anyone eats of this bread, he will live forever; and the bread also which I will give for the life of the world is My flesh." (John 6:48-51).

Jesus really did say "and not die." There are people who have not died and are still alive, hundreds and hundreds of years old. They are often called hermits or ancient ones, and they are somewhat changed by the process of living that long with God. I do not intend to die either; therefore I want everything in me removed that could cause me to do so. I take communion so that there is no death operating in me.

The plan of God is not for us to die and go to heaven; it is for us to have age-enduring life, living from the Kingdom of God within us. If we have unknowingly made a covenant with death, believing that we can only truly experience heaven after we die, we should break those agreements and mindsets. We can encounter God face to face now and become transformed into His likeness. The death and resurrection of Jesus have already overcome death, so we do not need to die. Jesus died our death on the cross so that we would not have to.

The power of Jesus' death and resurrection was so profound that on the day He arose, many tombs opened. Those whose bodies had been in them were resurrected and walked around Jerusalem, testifying to the power of His victory over death. Later on, Jesus breathed the breath of life into His disciples, imparting the life of God to them. Now, all of us who believe in Him have the life of God at work within us.

We have spiritualised it to avoid believing it. Not dying does not simply refer to life after physical death, but to a life that transcends death in this age and for all ages to come. The resurrection changed everything. Jesus made it possible for all of us to have a relationship with God and experience exactly the same quality of life that He has.

For My flesh is true food, and My blood is true drink. He who eats My flesh and drinks My blood abides in Me, and I in him. As the living Father sent Me, and I live because of the Father, so he who eats Me, he also will live because of Me.

This is the bread which came down out of heaven; not as the fathers ate and died; he who eats this bread will live forever." (John 6:55-58).

Jesus emphasises our intimate relationship with Him: those who eat His flesh and drink His blood abide in Him, and He in them. Communion initiates a deep connection and sustains life. It is unlike the manna the Israelites ate in the wilderness, which sustained them physically but could not prevent their eventual physical death. If breaking bread in an unworthy manner can lead to sickness and even physical death, then doing so in the right way can surely lead to life instead of death. Through communion, we access true food and true drink, the essence of Jesus' life, and we abide in Him.

Engaging with the cross through communion enables us to reverse the curse of death. By applying the body and blood of Jesus, we experience transformation, transfiguration, and metamorphosis (they are all the same Greek word). We are being transformed from mere human beings into living beings, reclaiming the divine image that Adam originally bore. This ongoing process of transformation is made possible through the truth of the law of the Spirit of life in Christ, which has set us free from the law of sin and death.

The law stipulated that if someone sinned, death was the consequence. The life, death and resurrection of Jesus have brought a new reality: we no longer need to face death. Forgiveness and redemption through Jesus have already dealt with the destructive power of sin, which damages us, harms others, and disrupts our relationship with God. We experience guilt, shame and condemnation as a result of sin. But when we align with God's truth that He has forgiven us, we receive the abundant life contained within the cross and the power of forgiveness. Death was the final enemy: its power is broken.

We are invited to partake in the divine nature, as Peter tells us in the opening remarks of his letter. We can not only escape the clutches of death but also shed everything within us that hinders our full manifestation as sons and daughters of

God. He holds a perfect picture of us within His thoughts, and through communion, we can engage with His DNA – the very essence of His being. Communion enables Him to transform us and align us with His perfect image of us.

When engaging in this by faith, I began to make declarations that align with this truth. Just this once, we are going to use them as I wrote them. I encourage you not merely to repeat them, but to use them as a foundation to put together your own declarations in your own words[5]. To fully experience the transformative power of declarations, we must speak with conviction as we actively embrace and engage in the process.

I strongly encourage you to listen to the recorded version of the activation at the end of this chapter, because in it I speak creative words into my DNA and release them into the atmosphere: those sound waves carry my intent. As I speak the words of my own declaration, allow them to resonate within you. The music playing in the background on the mp3 was specifically composed and recorded by Samuel Lane to contribute to restoration, and I again incorporate the use of crystal bowls, which carry and amplify the intent of the spoken word. Their sound waves can penetrate barriers, mindsets, belief systems, and even reach your DNA and soul, breaking free any blockages hindering your transformation.

As you partake in communion, allow these sound waves to embrace and surround you. Ideally, use loudspeakers rather than headphones, so that the sound waves can directly affect your whole body, not just your eardrums. Some sounds may resonate peacefully with you, while others may be more intense and penetrating. If a sound pierces through and penetrates deeply, do not retreat. Instead, choose to allow it open up whatever hindrance may be present, allowing the DNA of God and the frequency of His voice to bring life.

Embrace this process: whether you want to engage in your own heart, go into the realms of heaven, to the temple, or to

---

[5] Please see the resources page for two versions of the declarations

the blood of Jesus on the Mercy Seat. Let the frequency of God's voice resonate and bring you into agreement. When a higher frequency (such as God's love) encounters a lower one, it brings it into alignment. By engaging in communion, we can align our frequencies with the power of God's voice within His DNA, within the body and blood of Jesus. Picture this transformation taking place within your DNA, bringing life, purification and physical, spiritual and emotional change. Allow Him to deal with any traces of death within you. Embrace the freedom and life that God intends for you.

And it is not only sounds that have frequencies which hold the power to reach deep beneath the surface. If you diffuse essential oils, the fragrance of frankincense, for example, can cross the blood-brain barrier, reaching into your memory and enabling you to engage on a deeper level.

Remember, you have a choice in this process. Be open and receptive. Simply choose to engage, let the process unfold, and see where it leads. Actively choose to engage with the body and blood of Jesus, rather than just eating and drinking. You have the freedom to approach it in your own way and from any perspective you prefer: the key is to engage with faith and allow restoration to begin.

Take a moment now to prepare your bread and wine or whatever you choose to consume during communion.

Activation #4 Communion

As you partake of the body and blood of Jesus, I declare that you will experience eternal life and will not perish. Allow the truth of my words to resonate within you as you take communion. By doing so, you are engaging with the DNA of God and embracing the transformative power contained within the body and blood of Jesus. Let this power work within you, bringing transformation to

To stream the audio, scan the QR code or visit the resources page.

your soul and your physical body, right down to the level of your DNA.

If you are listening to the live audio mp3 recording, please speak these words with me as you listen. If not, I suggest you speak them aloud and meditate on them as you engage with communion:

> I eat your flesh and drink your blood
> so that I will not die but live forever.
>
> I engage in the DNA of God;
> I embrace the transforming power
> of the body and blood of Jesus.
>
> I engage the record containing the light, sound,
> and frequency of God's image for transfiguration.
>
> I embrace the record of the dimensions of the kingdom
> released in my body by the DNA of God.
>
> I engage that DNA record and apply it to my bones
> for health and wholeness
> to remove all negative epigenetic hereditary switches.
>
> I speak to my marrow
> and command it to be a new source of blood
> that will transform the DNA of my cells
> so that I can be transfigured and live forever.
>
> I apply the frequency of God's DNA to transform me
> into the image of Jesus.
>
> I command every genetic record to be transformed
> and my DNA to be re-sequenced
> into alignment with my eternal image.
>
> I apply the blood of Jesus
> to transform all impure genetic material
> – be transformed.
>
> I apply the blood of Jesus
> to all iniquitous genetic patterns
> – be cleansed.

COMMUNION

I call all my genetic material
to resonate with the DNA of God
and come into alignment with my eternal image.

I choose to bear the record of my eternal image,
conformed to the likeness
of my Father and Brother in heaven,
and to be transfigured to radiate their glory.

Let the breath of God be breathed into my life,
transforming me into a living being,
joined to the Lord and one spirit with Him.

I speak creative words to my DNA
to release the supernatural abilities of God.
I trigger the ability to see and move
in the spiritual realm of the kingdom.
I trigger the ability to transform matter
and control light and sound.

This process is not solely cognitive, but is about allowing these frequencies, vibrations, and words to resonate and echo within you, transforming, transfiguring and metamorphosing you into sonship. You are being restored and made whole, becoming the full image of who God created you to be.

Take the time to prepare your own declarations for future use: when you speak the words that God inspires you to speak, they will carry a frequency that penetrates you deeply, to bring about transformation. My own declarations were not created from my conscious mind but released from my spirit. You will get far deeper transformation by engaging with prayers and declarations which come from your own spirit joined to the Holy Spirit, and which resonate uniquely with you. For more information, see Mike's teaching series on Communion[6].

---

[6] Available separately or as part of the *Engaging God* programme, where you will find the 'Communion' sessions in Module 4.
Please visit eg.freedomarc.org/course/communion for the standalone 4-part series or eg.freedomarc.org/subscribe-to-engaging-god for the *Engaging God* free trial,

6. Redemptive Gifts

'How am I made?'

Some of the deepest and most significant questions people ask about themselves include:

'Who am I?'

'How am I made?'

'What is my purpose?'

God wants us to have a relationship with Him in which those answers are revealed to us. I now know who I am: I am a son of God. That is my identity, but if I did not know that in my heart, I would still be functioning on the basis of who I thought I was (or who someone else told me I was), and that was a very distorted image. Do you know that you are a son? I do not mean intellectual knowledge, but the knowledge that comes from revelation and experience. It is as we begin to see ourselves as God sees us that we can be transformed into that true image and come to that inner knowledge of our sonship. We looked at this in the previous book in this series, *Engaging the Father*.

But how am I made? That is a different question. How has God wired me to think, to feel and to act?

We have different gifts, according to the grace given to each of us. If your gift is prophesying, then prophesy in accordance with your faith; if it is serving, then serve; if it is teaching, then teach; if it is to encourage, then give encouragement; if it is giving, then give generously; if it is to lead, do it diligently; if it is to show mercy, do it cheerfully (Romans 12:6-8 NIV).

These seven gifts are quite different from the spiritual gifts or the five ministry gifts with which we might be more familiar, even where they have similar names. They have to do with personality; they are called 'redemptive' because they enable us to fulfil our role in redeeming creation, fulfilling God's plan for the restoration of all things. My redemptive gift is how I am wired to participate in that restoration.

The redemptive gifts are:

- Prophet
- Servant
- Teacher
- Exhorter
- Giver
- Ruler
- Mercy

Knowing God's purpose for our lives and answering His call allows us to make a difference in the world and bring glory to Him. Redemptive gifts are given to each of us, and when we align with them, we can become a gift to the body of Christ and play our part in restoring creation.

Positives and negatives

Each redemptive gift has a principle and a blessing associated with it. The principle represents how things are designed to work, whilst the blessing is the benefit that creation, society and other individuals receive from the gift. However, there are also some negatives associated with each gift.

Each redemptive gift also corresponds to a colour and is connected to one of the seven spirits of God, who are our heavenly tutors and trainers. Colours, sounds and fragrances in heaven are all in harmony with each other and can impact the earthly realm. Our spirits respond to frequencies beyond those the physical senses can perceive, so that we resonate with God's voice. As we engage with God in spirit, soul, and body, we begin to manifest heaven on earth and fulfil our true identity and destiny. The New Age movement and others have recognised the importance of frequency and resonance to our wellbeing, but the church has generally rejected it. When mature sons of God embrace these techniques in alignment with the Holy Spirit, they manifest righteousness, healing, and transformation.

Here is a brief outline of the qualities of each gift.

Prophets operate based on the principle of design, bringing about change. They have the ability to explore the boundaries of what is possible with God and lead others to fulfilment.
They tend to have a black-and-white worldview. They quickly discern things, but may struggle with moodiness and impatience.
Colour: red.
Seven spirits: Spirit of the Lord.

Servants carry the principle of authority and selflessly serves others. God trusts them to do only what He has asked them to do. They walk in holiness themselves and have a deep desire to empower others to achieve their best.
They will meet practical needs and show honour, but can struggle with self-worth and saying no.
Colour: orange.
Seven spirits: Spirit of Wisdom.

Teachers walk in responsibility and intimacy with God. They feel compelled to teach out of their own experience and so reveal God's presence to others.
They validate truth and show patience, but may be indecisive and struggle with confrontation.
Colour: yellow.
Seven spirits: Spirit of Understanding.

Exhorters follow the principle of sowing and reaping, using their own experiences to help others. An exhorter who has gone through pain and suffering is well placed to help others who are experiencing the same.
They relate well to others and look to nurture relationships, but can be manipulative and struggle with time management.
Colour: green.
Seven spirits: Spirit of Counsel.

Givers understand the principle of stewardship and bless others through generosity. They have the ability to be life-

givers and to think long-term.
They are independent, intuitive problem-solvers, but may struggle with faith and receiving.
Colour: blue.
Seven spirits: Spirit of Might.

Rulers pursue freedom and righteousness. They have the authority to release generational blessings and walk in spiritual dominion.
They manage time effectively, expect excellence, but can overlook their own faults and become self-centred.
Colour: indigo.
Seven spirits: Spirit of Knowledge.

Mercies are able to engage spirit to Spirit with God and find their highest fulfilment in that intimacy. They impart blessings to others and are able to transform the sinful into the holy.
They readily connect with others and provide a safe place; but often avoid confrontation, to the extent of tolerating abuse.
Colour: violet.
Seven spirits: Spirit of the Fear of the Lord.

Having a specific gift does not necessarily mean having all its associated strengths and weaknesses. Our expression of the gift may differ from others, as we will see. And maturity in faith enables us to develop strengths and overcome weaknesses[7].

Recognising and appreciating our own and others' gifts is crucial for effective collaboration in the body of Christ. We are not all the same, but God has called us together. As we learn to value the different gifts in each other we will receive the blessings and benefits that come with them. Yet how many of our churches function in ways that reward those who

---

[7] I go into much more detail in the teaching series Destiny: Redemptive Gifts: eg.freedomarc.org/course/destiny-redemptive-gifts
The seven blog posts based on that series contain many useful charts and diagrams, starting with freedomarc.blog/217-redemptive-gifts/

conform and marginalise those who do not? How would it be if instead we were to learn to prize distinctiveness rather than uniformity, as God does, and to see how beautiful our diversity can be in making us a 'whole church'?

Maturity and transformation require sacrifice and surrender. We are transformed as we present ourselves as living sacrifices and have our minds renewed. The process takes us from sacrifice through transformation to destiny. We focus on personal transformation while embracing the characteristics of other members of the body who exhibit different gifts, inviting those with complementary gifts and strengths to find their place alongside us. This fosters a community that honours and benefits from God's gifts in each other, a fully functioning body working together in harmony.

Why the negatives?

Each gift is associated with a demonic stronghold, a root of iniquity, and curses tied to our birthright. Some might wonder why there are weaknesses inherent in gifts. The presence of weaknesses in us means we have to learn to rely on others. They also provide opportunities for personal growth in maturity through triumph in times of difficulty. As James says,

Count it all joy, my brothers, when you meet various trials (James 1:2).

But if we allow our spirit to guide our soul and surrender to God's leading when something is exposed, we can always bring our issues to Him and allow Him to transform us. Whilst navigating change can be hard work, it is through overcoming difficulties that we mature.

Even if Adam and Eve had not deviated from the path of the tree of life, they would have faced obstacles. They would have grown into mature sons of God through overcoming, by drawing on their ongoing relationship with Him. The command to subdue was given right from the beginning, because God knew that would help us to develop and mature in sonship. They may have failed their tests: we get to pass them through Jesus. Yet we cannot overcome anything in our own strength, so it is essential for us to recognise and maintain our dependence on God.

If everything were always perfect, we could easily become complacent. Seasons of bliss may be followed by unexpected difficulties that serve to propel us into further transformation. Embracing this process with a healthy attitude brings joy and strength, making it easier to overcome the obstacles. Misery offers no strength to conquer anything.

Other factors

The seven redemptive gifts are received from birth and to some extent shape our lives, but other factors also influence how they are expressed, of which these are just a few:

> Parents' gifts have a significant impact on children's development, regardless of their own gifts.
>
> Birth order affects personality traits, with firstborns (for example) tending to be driven and perfectionistic.
>
> Maturity determines how gifts are expressed, particularly since immaturity emphasises the weaknesses of the gifts.
>
> Gender stereotypes hinder the acceptance of certain gifts.
>
> Wounds and coping mechanisms affect how gifts are expressed.
>
> Left-brained individuals approach gifts differently from right-brained individuals.
>
> Culture, time frame, and nationality shape how we perceive and express our gifts.
>
> Nations, regions, and churches to which individuals belong may also have their own redemptive gifts.

My redemptive gifts testimony

My redemptive gift is prophet/teacher. When I look at the world, I am looking to see how things work. In every situation I want to understand how it has come about and what has occurred. What can I learn? How can I explain that? What is behind that event? As a child, I was always inquisitive and loved taking things apart to discover how they worked. Of course, at five or six years old, I could not put most of them back together again. My mum was always pulling her hair out:

"You've broken it."
"I wanted to see how it worked."
"Well, now it doesn't work at all!"

Later, when I discovered movies, I was always drawn to tales of quests and adventures of discovery, because that is how I am made.

Our redemptive gift shapes the way we see and interact with the world, and therefore helps to determine the course of our lives. I may see things one way: someone else will experience the same situation or event and consider it through the lens of their own redemptive gift. And in the body of Christ we really need all seven perspectives, which create fullness.

Jesus is the fullness of all the redemptive gifts, and we would all say we desire to become more Christ-like. In that case, we may sometimes feel limited or defined by our redemptive gift, but that is just our soul's natural thinking. As we become conformed to His image we will demonstrate more of the gifts; but initially each of us has a primary and a secondary gift, shaping how we think, feel, and act by default. We did not have to learn it; it is just how we are. This gift is put into us at conception, into our soul. When Adam became a living being or a living soul, he was created with a redemptive gift.

Of course, we have sometimes unlearned it, rejected it, or had it damaged. The enemy would always like to rob us of our redemptive gift because it is the particular way we are wired that enables us to engage effectively in restoring creation.

God intends us to be involved in that restoration as sons, as co-heirs and co-creators with Jesus (and when creation is restored, to be involved in creating something else).

All of us are creative in some way, whether we recognise it or not, since we are all made in God's image. Some will express creativity in art, poetry or music, some in science, industry, commerce or other ways. That creativity within us derives from the image of God in us. But ultimately, He wants us to be doing the things that Jesus did (and greater ones). I may know how to do some of those things, and I have seen others done, but I am not living that way all the time. Mostly, in those instances, He was showing me what is possible if we are willing to pursue and continue the journey.

Knowing how God designed each of us individually is crucial, in order to fulfil the purpose for which we were created. But how would we feel if, having shown us our redemptive gift, God then denied us the opportunity to exercise it? How would we perceive ourselves? For instance, if God made you to be a servant but then restricted you from serving, and your identity was closely tied to serving, how would that make you feel? Why would God do such a thing? Because if we find ourselves unable to 'do', it reveals whether our identity was firmly rooted in Him, as sons of our Father, or was based on what we do. That is what happened to me. God created me with a specific purpose; but I was using the gifts He bestowed on me to find my identity, so He decided to call a halt to my activities for a period of time. I was extremely unhappy with that; I found it intensely challenging. Nevertheless, as David said,

I will give thanks to You,
because I am awesomely and wonderfully made;
Wonderful are Your works,
And my soul knows it very well (Psalm 139:14).

In this context, the term 'soul' refers not to the mind or emotions, but to something deep within the core of our being. My core being understood well who I am, whereas my mind and my emotions struggled to grasp my true identity.

I gradually began to realise how precious God's thoughts were (and are) towards me. His thoughts are vast, and initially I could not believe what He was saying. It made no sense to me. He persisted, and still I resisted.

Therefore humble yourselves under the mighty hand of God, so that He may exalt you at the proper time (1 Peter 5:6).

Eventually, I gave up resisting and said, "Okay, if this is who You say I am, I agree." Even though what He was saying about me seemed like too much, too good to be true, that was an act of humility. Submitting to the mighty hand of God enables Him to elevate you to the position He always intended.

You may think that does not sound very humble. But pride is the opposite of humility, and pride would be rejecting the identity God had given me, thinking I knew better than Him. And for a while that is what I was doing – disagreeing with God and rejecting His view of me as His son. Some of it was not conscious, but it became more explicit over time. I struggled to accept and embrace the truth. Eventually, God brought me to the realisation that my soul was not aligned with my spirit. Although my spirit was thriving and capable of governing my life, I had yet to surrender fully. There were certain areas where my soul held power that I could not overcome: not sin, but rather issues related to my identity. I did not truly know who I was. I had been involved in ministry activities and positions of church leadership for years, but it was not coming from a place of authentic identity. I was 'doing' to establish my identity. Once I discovered my redemptive gifts, it was easy to see where that came from.

Discovering redemptive gifts

On the resources webpage, you will find links to some redemptive gift questionnaires and surveys. We have used them and found them helpful, at least in beginning to understand where our gifts might lie, but they are not definitive. As with any questionnaire, the results can easily be skewed by (consciously or unconsciously) providing what we consider the 'right' answers.

Arthur Burk, the leading authority on this subject, does not advocate using surveys, which he claims are 60% accurate at best. Instead, he discovered his own redemptive gift by immersing himself in the qualities of each gift and attempting to think and act as if they were his own. He assigned each gift to a day of the week and imagined himself as a particular person of his acquaintance with that gift, each on their respective day. He tried to understand their perspectives and to approach problems from their unique angles. Through this exercise, he gained deep insights into all the gifts and eventually identified his own:

> I was able to definitively determine my gift, because it was so easy to be the one person, that one day. No matter whether I was grocery shopping, mowing the lawn, reading a book or being a dad, it was simple to step into that one persona. Each of the other six was a learned discipline which did not resonate with who I really was[8].

So please feel free to take one or more of the questionnaires, or use Arthur's method (which, as he acknowledges, requires a good deal more time and effort than simply taking a test). Perhaps you already know your redemptive gift or gifts. Whatever your results may be, from whatever method, I encourage you to review them from time to time. You may indeed know who God has made you to be, but you can always reassess where you currently stand in relation to that, and reflect on how you would feel about yourself if you were not engaged in activities associated with your gifting.

God challenged someone I knew who exhibited the ruler gift not to exercise authority. This raised the question of their identity: If they were made to rule but could not, who were they then? Similarly, I met a prophetic person who would often ask the same questions I did, because our wiring was so similar. It was amusing to recognise myself in what they

---

[8] Arthur Burk: theslg.com/content/redemptive-gifts-test
Accessed June 8th 2023.

asked. This kind of reflection is essential for our growth and maturity.

If you use the questionnaires, try to avoid overanalysing the questions: trust your initial instincts. There really are no right or wrong responses, and it is not about achieving a perfect score out of 100. They are simply intended to provide a measure of insight into your thinking and reactive tendencies, which may or may not accurately reflect your redemptive gift.

I will share my own results as an example: they turned up three gifts that scored quite similarly. The first two, you know about already. Number one was prophet (and please note that it does not refer to prophesying or spiritual gifts, but is about how I perceive the world, seeing it through the lens of a prophet). The second gift was that of teacher, and it was nearly equal to the prophet score. But lastly, it suggested I had the gift of ruler. I was sufficiently aware to know that it was through necessity that I had learned how to function in that. It was not innate for me. So when someone came and joined the church leadership team who had the ruler gift, it was a relief because I no longer had to continue doing things the way I had been doing them. I could embrace who I truly was, rather than trying to be a jack-of-all-trades. That is the beauty of individuals expressing their redemptive gifts when working as a team. Understanding each other's gifts can enable us to honour and support one another more effectively.

We are all at different levels of maturity, and God loves us regardless. However, we cannot fully function as His sons until we mature. Whilst we can operate in lordship within the heavenly realms, seated on thrones and exercising a level of authority, the extent of that authority corresponds to the holiness in our lives. God would not grant me the authority of a king or a chancellor, among other roles I am called to fulfil, until He had addressed the issue of my redemptive gift and how I was improperly exercising it to affirm my identity. Once I was set free from that, everything changed. My entire life took on a completely different dimension, with revelation and authority that I did not even know existed.

Until we are fully mature, our redemptive gift is likely to manifest both the positive and negative aspects. Losing track of time is a weakness that I used to get frustrated with in others because it is not something I struggle with. I manage my time quite effectively. When I questioned why someone had not accomplished a seemingly simple task in the time available, they might reply that something else was more important. Instead of being frustrated, I have now learned to be more considerate of people's priorities. By honouring and appreciating others for who they are, I can encourage them and receive the benefits of their unique qualities.

We cannot expect others to be like us and behave exactly as we would. No one else will do things exactly as we would; we need to trust people to do things their way and encourage them to be themselves. As we mature, we will begin to display elements of all seven gifts. However, for now, our focus is on understanding who we are meant to be and how our soul's desire for independence may hinder that. As we surrender our soul's control, it does not mean we cease to be ourselves. Instead, it enables us to embrace all the different gifts, as we are all called to serve one another.

My redemptive gift is not a get-out clause for avoiding doing something. For example, exhorting and encouraging one another are vital aspects of our journey. Whilst it may not be my primary gifting, in a one-on-one situation where someone needs encouragement, I cannot simply send them away or act as if it is not my responsibility. The Holy Spirit can guide me to operate like Jesus in that particular situation, and to encourage them, because that is what they need.

Ultimately, we are to become fully developed individuals, conformed to the image of sonship, just as Jesus is the Son of God. We are all on a journey towards that goal. Along the way, I have observed personal growth in areas where I am now more compassionate than I used to be. I can recognise how someone is feeling and offer them the best help I can by being myself and allowing the Holy Spirit to guide me. It is not my own soul directing my actions, but rather me embracing who

I am. When we get together, we can all encourage and support each other in our unique gifting; whilst we are all moving towards the full likeness of Jesus, we acknowledge that it is a process and we each have our own journey.

As we become conformed to the image of Jesus, we will display the character and essence of sonship, as well as physical attributes such as immortality and a resurrected body unaffected by death. Our transformation involves bearing the characteristics of God. We are sons of God, not sons of Adam.

I see wonderful diversity in the people I meet: we are not mere clones. Every individual is unique, and each of us is undergoing personal growth and transformation. We all start from a different point and have distinct life experiences that shape us. If all of us can show grace and patience to one another in this journey, that will be indicative of the fruit of the Spirit operating in our lives. To look at one another and recognise a son of God is a profound experience. It allows us to gain a broader perspective on people and cultivate appreciation for them, fostering a culture of honour in which everyone can thrive and be authentic.

Religious expectation often pressurises us to imitate others. We may find ourselves thinking, "If only I were like Bob Jones, or Kathryn Kuhlman." But such remarkable individuals were just as imperfect as us, and went through a similar transformative process. Even if they have passed on, they continue their growth and learning in another realm. The process does not end when we join the men in white linen; there is always room for further maturing. Embracing our uniqueness frees us from comparing ourselves to others. We respect and honour one another's differences and together, as the body of Christ, we see things from His perspective.

Our journey requires the involvement of other people and their unique gifts. Recognising our need for others helps us maintain humility. Paul's "thorn in the flesh" served as a reminder to keep his feet on the ground: even as his spirit soared in heavenly realms, a reminder to earth it out in this realm.

Conclusion

Redemptive gifts are the way God has wired each of us to be. They can point us towards personal fulfilment and effective contribution in our relationships with others in the ekklesia and in wider society. The life we have lived and the experiences we have had can mask or reveal our redemptive gifting, but ultimately our basic personality type is still there. We may try to fight against it, for all kinds of reasons, but eventually we will find it simpler to surrender to the way He has designed us to be rather than attempt to function independently from it. As we do, our redemptive gifts can empower us to fulfil our destiny.

By engaging our spirits and following the guidance of the Holy Spirit, we can discover our true identities, gifts, and destinies and help others to find theirs. This allows God to transform us all and enables us to participate in the redemption of all creation. However, even our strengths can conceal potential pitfalls. If we are using how God made us to frame our identity, He cannot release us into the reality of who we truly are. He always wants to bless and empower us, but if we cling to false identities, He will bless us first of all by addressing the issues. When in chapter 15 we come to the separating of our soul and spirit, all this can be something you surrender if you need to.

7. The Dance Floor

Hebrew marriage

As we saw in chapter 2, there are five components of the Hebrew marriage process. *Lakah*, which is the garden, then *Segullah*, the dance floor. Third is the *Mikvah*, the soaking room. *Ketubah* represents the contract, the terms and conditions of the marriage covenant. This is the point that triggered everything for me. Without the right perspective, the *Ketubah* could become very performance-driven, leading us to make demands on God, whilst trying to live up to His expectations.

And then finally we have the *Huppah*, the covering of the cloud of God's presence, also known as the glory cloud or the dark cloud. They are essentially different perspectives of the same thing, and lead us to the bridal chamber, where the co-creation inherent in the marriage relationship can take place. It is a level of intimacy that surpasses anything else I have experienced.

It was not until 2016, four years after God first told us that we would have a marriage ceremony for the church here, that I even began to teach about the *Ketubah*. It had taken us four years to get to that point. I had learned a lot in those four years, because as a forerunner I had to go through it personally before I could teach it. Eventually, as a church, we were willing to let go of our independence, and were able to hold a marriage ceremony.

I am not saying this has to take you four years, but please take your time working through the remainder of this book, and do not try to finish it in one or two days. In the intensive event where I first taught this material, people did only have three days, so make use of the extra time you have as a reader.

I highly encourage you to follow through step by step, without getting stuck on any particular point, as they are all just a part of the journey towards the bridal chamber, where we find the joy of Jesus bringing us into a whole new level of experience.

In John 14, Jesus talks about preparing a place for us, which references this marriage agreement. Reading that passage without understanding the concept of Hebrew marriage has led many to a completely mistaken interpretation. When Jesus says, "Behold, I go and prepare a place for you," those are the words a bridegroom would say to the bride during the betrothal. The bride would eagerly ask when he would return to take her to that place, and the bridegroom would reply, "When the place of preparation is ready and the father releases me to come." Their house would be built attached to the groom's father's house.

Jesus was emphasising the intimacy of our relationship. He was not talking about going to heaven when we die or inviting us to join Him in magnificent mansions there. We are the dwelling place of God. He went to the cross to prepare us to be a place where He can reside. On the day of resurrection, He returned to demonstrate that He is in the Father, we are in Him, and He is in us. This entire discourse in John 14 revolves around the context of marriage and intimacy.

The garden is where intimacy begins, where we find restored identity and sonship, not relying on our works. In the garden, we do not have to strive and work hard but rest in His presence. Whilst we can plant testimonies and cultivate the soil, it is done from a place of rest, not from a place of striving.

The garden is a place of peace and tranquility where we can experience the love and acceptance of God. As we sit in the green pastures, He looks into our eyes and tells us how wonderful we are. He expresses His love for us and desires to have an intimate relationship with each one of us. He has looked into our eyes and told us, "I want you." This is the *Lakah*, the proposal, the moment He asks us to be His own.

If you have never heard God say these words to you, spend more time in the green pastures. Engage with Him, look into His face, and gaze into His eyes, where you will see the love, desire and passion He has for you. It is a beautiful thing to hear these words and know that you are so special to Him.

Our worth is not self-worth: it comes from the value that God gives us when He says, "I have chosen you to be mine."

Next is *Segullah*, the dance floor, where He tells us "You are My treasured possession". In this chapter, we will explore the dance floor and its deepening levels of intimacy and connection in our relationship with God.

Flow

Our desire in all this is to allow the river of life to flow from our innermost being out into the world, bringing forth abundant life wherever we go. To some extent, at least, that is already happening, but there is room for greater expansion. Most of us are still operating within a limited sphere; but God's plan is for us to extend our reach from Jerusalem to Judea, Samaria, and the ends of the earth. God is continuously expanding what He is doing in us because He has designed us to be a conduit of heaven's flow into the earth.

Look again at the gates image on the resources webpage. Within our spirit, there is the gate of first love, which we open and allow the flow to begin in us as we worship God in agreement and surrender. Sometimes familiar spirits can block this flow, sitting outside our spirit gates and hindering the process. They may have access due to our involvement in religious activity, ritual and superstition, often counterfeits of what God truly desires. For instance, the gate of the fear of God is intended to help us honour and revere God, since we would never wish to do anything that would bring dishonour to Him. However, this can become legalistic when it turns into fear-based obligation. Familiar spirits will intensify this if we give them opportunity, leading to a life driven by fear of making mistakes or of somehow disappointing God.

In this marriage preparation, He will help us remove these familiar spirits and address obstacles which impede the flow, so that the river of life is able to reach the dance floor, the soaking room and eventually the bridal chamber, for the consummation of the marriage.

Thanks to my curious nature, I stumble upon most of the things I share by accident, or you could say serendipity. One day, I had a thought, "Where does this river go?" So I got in and started floating downstream. After a while I asked Him, "Where is this?" And He said, "This is the dance floor."

While I am not generally considered a good dancer, it does not matter to me: I express myself before God, not people. In the past I was self-conscious about how I appeared to others, but that changed in the early nineties when God knocked the British reserve out of me. In a men's meeting it seemed that God wanted us to be more expressive and passionate in our worship, so someone picked up a huge pillow with a Union Flag on it and declared, "I'm going to knock the British stuffing out of all of you!" He proceeded to whack us all with the pillow, really hard. If I had known how to do cartwheels, I would have done them right then and there. I felt so free! Since that moment, I am completely free to express joy and celebration before God. That was part of Him unblocking and dealing with the hindrances and restrictions within me.

The four chambers of the heart are all about engaging with God and enabling positive transformation into the image of Jesus. He wants to bring us all into freedom, so we can all be ourselves and engage Him unconcerned by what others think.

Treasures of darkness

"I will give you the treasures of darkness
And hidden wealth of secret places,
So that you may know that it is I,
The LORD, the God of Israel, who calls you by your name..."
(Isaiah 45:3).

There are treasures concealed for us in darkness. And on the dance floor, there are light and dark areas, in a checkerboard pattern. Initially, when I started dancing there, I avoided stepping on any of those dark areas, the black parts, and I would not let God guide me onto them. Not that I resisted, exactly, but I just did not want to dance on those black squares. I had a feeling that there was something unknown inside them, and apparently I did not fully trust God to the extent I thought I did. If I had truly surrendered and allowed Him to lead me, I would have gone wherever He led.

Still, I was more drawn to the illuminated areas, where things already revealed were made even clearer. I experienced deeper revelation as God revealed Himself to me in a profound way. It was as if His light surrounded me as I danced: it was like dancing with streams of light. Every time I stepped into the light, I felt the presence of God. It was as if strands of His divine essence were intertwining around me, transforming me into His image by revealing Himself to me. I absolutely loved being on the dance floor.

Eventually, once my soul and spirit were separated, I was able to step onto the dark areas as well. I knew there were hidden mysteries in that darkness, waiting to be discovered. I no longer feared the darkness because by then I had been through the dark cloud. Even in the darkness, there is illumination: within it lie revelations and unveiled mysteries that come to light when we embrace them.

The dance floor is where we begin to take on the image of sonship by engaging with the character, nature and essence of God. On the dance floor we get to know Father, Son and Spirit intimately, experiencing their fragrance, frequency, and unique characteristics. They are indeed all God, but they also display distinct qualities that create a personal and intimate connection. Through engaging with each of them, we become intertwined with their light in a beautiful, transforming dance.

On the dance floor of our hearts we can engage with the eternal record of our identity, the song of all songs. This record describes who we are in God's eyes. I find great joy and delight as the light of God surrounds me and initiates transformation. I am being transfigured and transformed by the light, which effectively brings my two human strands of DNA into alignment with my third light strand, the one that carries my eternal record. I am being conformed to the image of who I truly am, my new creation self, aligning with the characteristics of God. However, this requires addressing the genealogy of the other two strands, most effectively in taking communion. Through engaging with the nine characteristics of God I become aligned with His image, and this alignment profoundly impacts and changes me.

There are various ways to experience the dance floor, where this intimacy and alignment can happen. We can be immersed in the depths of the Father, Son and Spirit, taking us to a whole different level of connection. We can be clothed with Father, Son and Holy Spirit, with the armour of light, of righteousness, and the whole armour of God. Such experiences help us become who we truly are in Him.

The dance floor is not a one-size-fits-all formula that guarantees specific experiences at certain times. Rather, it is a journey that continually unfolds according to the seasons and circumstances of our lives. Sometimes we instantly connect with a revelation or experience, while at other times it may be released to us gradually. When we consume food, our bodies release immediate nutrients, providing instant energy. However, other nutrients are gradually released into our bloodstream as digestion continues. In just the same way, as we engage with the Spirit, some revelations may have an immediate impact, whilst others unfold over time.

We cannot impose a fixed timeline or try to rationalise everything cognitively. It is better simply to receive and allow the experiences to unfold in their proper season. Even if we do not fully comprehend what is happening in the moment, we can trust that the deeper levels of revelation and transformation will be made available to us as we progress.

Dance with me

Preconceived ideas of how God will manifest can cause us to miss out on what He is doing. The different faith streams we come from may have different views of what a spiritual experience looks like. Some may regard falling to the floor as a sign of encountering God, whilst others may reject that altogether. Experiencing God's presence is not limited to a specific set of actions, reactions or sensations. Whether we see, feel or sense anything, our spirits will receive what God imparts to us.

God eagerly awaits as you step onto the dance floor, whether or not you can currently perceive it. On the dance floor you can engage with God, and He will respond as you engage with faith and desire. Although it may take some time to develop the ability to see and engage more easily, He still welcomes and embraces you. If you find seeing and engaging with God challenging, do not be discouraged; that does not mean you are not receiving anything. Stay open to His presence.

As we embrace the character and nature of God, we step onto the dance floor and begin to take on the image of sonship. It is like being surrounded by the light of God. Light carries the potential for manifesting into reality. We typically perceive light as particles (called photons), but it can also behave as waves that eventually manifest when observed. Quantum physics tells us it is only when something is observed that it becomes part of our reality.

Therefore, when we actively engage with God, something significant occurs. Without our engagement, nothing happens: we have not activated the potential for that experience. By expressing your desire to engage more intimately with God's character and nature on the dance floor of your heart, you open yourself up to His presence. Even if you have never been there before, do not worry. If you have already been engaging with God, you have likely dealt with any reservations or concerns, but if not, simply engage with faith. Desire to engage with God intimately. You are His treasured possession: He values you highly, and will reveal Himself to you.

As you engage with God, you may experience His presence through revelation, vibrational frequencies, songs, or other kinds of encounters. Some feel as if they are immersed in a song, and that song encompasses their lives. Personally, when we sing the Jesus Culture song *Dance With Me*, I perceive it as God singing His song of my life over me. I step onto the dance floor and am enveloped by His song, which transforms me as I receive and embrace it. Others may experience God's presence more through light, or any number of different perceptions: in my case, it is a combination of light and song.

Whatever your experience may be, embrace it, as it will bring a transformative and aligning energy around you. For me, dancing with God is a deeply romantic experience. I love dancing with Him, but I am not particularly fond of dancing with other people, though I may love them dearly.

A little lower?

What is man that You think of him,
And a son of man that You are concerned about him?
Yet You have made him a little lower than God,
And You crown him with glory and majesty!
You have him rule over the works of Your hands;
You have put everything under his feet...
(Psalm 8:4-6).

Psalm 8 beautifully expresses the significance of humanity in God's eyes. We are created a little lower than God, crowned with glory and majesty. On the dance floor, we are brought into His glory and majesty, discovering our true identity as His sons and daughters. It is not that God lowers Himself to our level; He elevates us to His. He reveals Himself to us, allowing us to see who we are in relation to Him. Ultimately, it is by the glory of our sonship that creation is to be set free.

Religious people sometimes feel uncomfortable with this because they believe only God can possess such glory. But in Romans 8, Paul explicitly tells us that creation will be set free into the freedom of the glory of the children of God. If we recognise that we were originally crowned with glory, that Adam was clothed in light, his spirit around his body, then we can also see that our spirit and physical body need to be restored to their original state. This is where transfiguration comes into play, as we are clothed with the glory of our spirit in light, not just our physical bodies. God wants to lift us up to a place of sonship, where everything will be under our authority, and we will rule as He always intended.

Fire stones

When I am on the dance floor in heaven, I am engaging with the fire stones. These are nine (and eventually twelve) stones or steps leading up to God's throne, on which we can connect with our identity. They align with the nine stones on Lucifer's body, the twelve stones on the high priest's breastplate and the twelve stones of the New Jerusalem.

Lucifer, as the covering cherub, was responsible for releasing the light of sonship into the world. Ezekiel 28 tells us that he walked on the stones of fire in Eden, the Garden of God. If he had not chosen to leave his position, he would have enabled us to engage with God by revealing His nature through light.

However, God has restored what was lost, and I have personally experienced the transformative power of engaging with the fire stones many times. Each engagement offers a different level of experience, and it usually takes a year or longer for my soul to fully comprehend and catch up with the revelations I have received. They have been extraordinarily transformative for me, and can be for you too[9].

The song of our DNA

Our DNA possesses a unique melody, a song that resonates within us, but it is currently aligned with our two strands of DNA. There is a computer program that can translate your DNA into a musical composition. You can even send a sample of your DNA to a university lab, where they can decipher its sequences and (for a fee) produce a song that is your very own. However, before you try anything like that, I believe your DNA will benefit from undergoing transformation. I am more interested in the song encoded within my light strand, which

---

[9] I described my fire stones encounters at length in my previous book, *Engaging the Father*. If you have not done so already, I encourage you to read it or listen to the corresponding conference teaching set; it complements this *Dark Cloud* material and provides further background, support and guidance.

holds the power to align my entire being with it. In fact, our individual songs, our scrolls of destiny written in eternity, are intended to blend into the symphony of creation and the heavenly chorus.

I love engaging in that. I recall a moment when I found myself in the Father's garden years ago. I was just floating there, as He was not allowing me to engage in any activity. My sole purpose was to be present and observe. I was suspended in the air, rocking gently, and feeling weightless, as if I were a part of the atmosphere. In that moment, every particle of my being seemed to explode and harmonise with the song of creation, resonating with what was and what is. This inspired me to pursue the restoration of creation, so that I might hear again the beautiful symphony that once emanated from everything, in which all our songs blended harmoniously.

Our songs have a profound impact on creation itself. When we align ourselves with our true song, we begin to influence and shape our surroundings: creation responds to us, and everything falls into place beautifully. He is the lover of our souls, and when we sing, it becomes a powerful expression of love. It is the song of all songs, unique to each one of us. Therefore, when you step onto the dance floor, allow your song to guide you. It may or may not have words; mine does not, but its notes create patterns that resonate with my very essence, making me feel at one with them.

In this dance, there is a romantic connection: He sees Himself in me, revealing who He always intended me to be. It is about becoming one. It is an invitation to deepen our relationship with Him, to experience intimacy, and to embrace His desire for us as His treasured possession. This love song, this eternal romance, beckons us to engage with God on a profound level. Our destiny aligns with our spirit in eternity, and this song is embedded within God's very own DNA.

God's DNA

As we have seen, the cherub's covering had nine stones, representing nine aspects of God. The number nine represents completeness, as it remains unchanged when added to or multiplied with itself: it always produces nine, as in 18 (1+8=9) or 81 (8+1=9). The breastplate of the High Priest, however, had twelve stones, looking forward to the New Jerusalem and representing the fullness of government in which we are united with God. He has chosen to include mankind in His government and establish a father-child relationship with us: His nine strands combined with our three.

The Father's three DNA strands are judgment, justice and holiness. When we engage with Him, we receive the fullness of these attributes. My perspective on judgment, justice and holiness have been revolutionised, leading me to understand their expression in us through patience, kindness and goodness, the fruit of the Spirit. These attributes inform all of His interactions with us and are revealed, both in creation and our lives, through His precepts, statutes and laws.

The strands of Jesus' DNA are the way, the truth and the life, reflected in us as love, joy and peace, and outworked through the ordinances, judgments, and commandments of God. Understanding the unconditional nature of God's love and allowing it to flow through us is essential when administering His kingdom. Otherwise, we tend to operate in the flesh, leading to the kind of negative judgment found in dogmatic arguments, rather than simply extending God's love to all.

The Holy Spirit's three strands are righteousness, peace and joy, reflected as faithfulness, gentleness and self-control, and manifested through His testimonies, ways and wonders. As we engage on the dance floor of our hearts, these attributes are imparted to us by revelation through experience.

Light and mysteries

So, what is it like to be on the dance floor? It is a realm of awe-inspiring light and mysteries. As we dance with Him, hidden things come into the light. He unveils mysteries that had been concealed in darkness, those treasures spoken of by Isaiah, hidden within secret places, just waiting to be discovered. Some things are so deep that you cannot even see them until you step into them.

It is the glory of God to conceal a matter,
But the glory of kings is to search out a matter.
(Proverbs 25:2).

We are those kings. However, we cannot expect to grasp everything in a single dance: we have to keep returning for more. It is a continual process of stepping onto squares of darkness and light, receiving revelation and experience; God inviting and drawing us into the depths of His mysteries.

Engaging in this dance can be an extraordinary, almost psychedelic experience, transcending our usual encounters and even surpassing other heavenly experiences. It unlocks lost supernatural abilities still stored within our DNA, abilities lost at the fall, at the flood or at Babel; enabling us to manifest and control the light, sound, and vibrational energies necessary for performing miracles.

Activation #5 Dance floor

Again, I would encourage you to relax. Do not strive to see, relax; allow whatever happens to happen, and your spirit will engage. If you engage beyond that into cognitive revelation, that is awesome. Just go with it.

To stream the audio, scan the QR code or visit the resources page.

> When we open our first love gate,
> as we have,
> and we invite God's presence,
> He can lead us.
>
> So as you close your eyes,
> we have already opened that door,
> so it's just a matter of stepping back through.
>
> When that door is open,
> we can invite God's presence
> and we can allow God's presence to envelop us,

to flood all around us,
so that His presence begins to activate around us.
Then just let Him lead us
to follow the river of life
to flow through the garden of our heart
to flow onto the dance floor.

Let the river take you there.
Sometimes there is a journey to get there.
Go with the flow of the journey.
Sometimes you are almost instantly there.
If you have been there before,
it is easy to step back into that place.

Allow Him to embrace you in the dance.

Allow Him to take the lead.
And allow His light,
His characteristics
to flow around you;
His song,
and your song,
To come around you.

Let it empower you,
transform you,
take you into mysteries,
unveil your DNA,
coming out of eternity.

Just dance with Him.

Sometimes when you are on the dance floor, you will find the seven spirits of God, because they are mandated to bring you into sonship; and their colours will begin to dance around you.

So sometimes you sense colour.
You sense a sound
and a fragrance
and a different frequency.
Allow that to begin to impart...

This is another place you can visit in the night watch, dancing with God on the dance floor. It is an ongoing process, not something you simply do once. Every time you reengage, something new and fresh unfolds. God is infinite, and we can never fully engage with every aspect of Him on just one occasion. It is truly extraordinary whenever we engage, but there is always more to discover.

Even if you feel you have not really experienced anything, know that your spirit has engaged, and that will bring about change. Allow it to take root and bear fruit, because it is the fruit that matters, rather than just the experience itself. These experiences are wonderful, but the real key lies in the transformation they bring to our lives, which can take weeks, months, or even years to fully manifest. But that is perfectly fine: stick with it – this journey is a marathon, not a sprint.

8. The Soaking Room

Therefore I urge you, brothers and sisters, by the mercies of God, to present your bodies as a living and holy sacrifice, acceptable to God, which is your spiritual service of worship. And do not be conformed to this world, but be transformed by the renewing of your mind, so that you may prove what the will of God is, that which is good and acceptable and perfect (Romans 12:1-2).

In this chapter we are moving on into the soaking room, and exploring its role in preparing us for a deeper relationship with God. Here Paul urges his readers not to be conformed to the world, which implies that the world is likely to have influenced us to some extent. Another version says, "Don't let the world around you squeeze you into its own mould[10]" whilst the literal versions will point out that it is 'this age' rather than 'this world'. The Mirror Bible renders the phrase as 'current religious tradition', emphasising the overriding religious influences prevalent in that society at the end of the Old Covenant age.

Our own external programming may derive from nature, nurture, or trauma, and probably a mixture of all these. Each has impacted us, and God desires to undo their effects. He wants to engage us in a way that allows His presence to flow, and saturates us with fragrance, oil and life. This is a crucial aspect of the marriage preparation.

Romans 8:29 tells us that we have been predestined to conform to God's image. God has already determined this desired outcome, but how it unfolds depends on our choices. He has given us the opportunity to cooperate with Him: we can either embrace it and pursue it, or resist it. He is working to eventually draw everyone into voluntarily agreeing to be conformed to His original will and purpose. He is at work in every individual, bringing them into a relationship with Him; but we have the opportunity to cooperate here and now.

---

[10] The New Testament in Modern English by J.B. Phillips, 1960.

In Peter's sermon, recorded in Acts 3:20-21, he mentions the period of the restoration of all things, a period in which I believe we are currently living. It began when Jesus came, restoring all things (including us), and it is continuing. For now, our own restoration will be our primary focus: if we are not restored, creation cannot be fully restored. Our own restoration as sons must be our priority so that creation can respond to our sonship. God wishes to restore us to our original condition and purpose, not to a lesser purpose or a degraded state. He wants to restore us to the way He always intended us to be. If we cooperate, our own 'all things' (that is, all aspects of ourselves) will be restored. This process can be accelerated if we embrace it, and that is the purpose of this book.

Preparation

The soaking room is one element of this restoration within the chambers of our hearts. It is a place of engagement where God wants to bring us into restriction. That may seem strange, even undesirable, but it is in this place that the best things can happen to us. If being placed in a cocoon and having the heat turned up can accelerate the process, so much the better. Some aspects of this may feel like a struggle, like a butterfly trying to break out of its cocoon; but remember that if you help the butterfly out, its wings may never gain the strength needed for flight. It may be intensely challenging and difficult, as if we are restricted or in a 'dark cloud'. However, such seasons present opportunities for growth.

The soaking room serves as a preparation space for the soul and body to be able to radiate God's glory as children of light. We soak in the frequencies of God: sound, light, fragrance, oil, healing balm and life itself. Here, our bodies can undergo transformation as well as our souls, leading to health, wholeness and the activation of the full abilities encoded in our DNA.

In context of the five aspects of a Hebrew marriage, we are now in the *Mikvah* or preparation stage. This lasted three days, as seen in the biblical example of the Israelites before receiving the Ten Commandments (we will explore that further when we consider the *Ketubah*). If we desire a closer connection with Him, deeper levels of relationship and intimacy, it will be good to actively engage in this preparation. You do have a choice: resist or engage. The longer you resist, the longer it takes; to move forward you eventually have to give up and surrender. I resisted: you do not need to repeat my mistake. This time of preparation is essential to experiencing the intimacy and deeper relationship we all desire.

Water and fire

When you pass through the waters, I will be with you;
And through the rivers, they will not overflow you.
When you walk through the fire, you will not be scorched,
Nor will the flame burn you (Isaiah 43:2).

The prophet is clear that we can expect to encounter both water and fire in our journey. When we embrace the soaking room, we can engage with the water in the river of life and the fire in the river of fire, extremely different experiences. Before diving into the fire, it is best to be well-soaked in the water. So in the rest of this chapter we will focus on soaking in the river of life and what it represents, and in the next we will go on to engage in the fire.

Any aspects of our identities we have derived from external or earthly perspectives will be challenged, especially our view of ourselves and any other limiting attitudes and beliefs. Such mindsets conceal who we really are as sons of God, made in His image. He will expose the lies and dispel the limitations, freeing us from the need to identify and remove them ourselves. Naturally, our focus will always be on what we want to avoid. If you ask me not to think of a tree, I will inevitably think of a tree – in the very effort to not think of one! Instead, we can allow the truth to transform us.

True transformation occurs when we allow new ways of thinking to completely reshape our minds. Then the old ways fall away and there is no room for them: even if they try to creep back in, we now see them as obvious lies and wonder how we ever believed as we did. We cannot try to transform ourselves through our own efforts. Instead, let us surrender ourselves as living sacrifices, and allow Jesus, our High Priest, to transform us. Embracing the soaking room is vital to this.

However, it is not only about removing the lies, but also about unveiling new truths and possibilities we would never have anticipated. I experienced extraordinary encounters even while I was still transitioning back and forth between heaven and earth, but there was a ceiling on my experiences because I was constantly shifting in and out. It was quite a high ceiling: I was ruling on a mountain, seated on a throne, operating as a lord – but God wanted to take me to another level.

My soul, still wired to 'need to know' what was happening, would not allow my spirit to remain engaged without being aware itself. My spirit was tethered to my soul, hindering me from reaching the fullness of my potential and restricting me from realising possibilities that have since become a lifestyle. That is why the tethering needs to be severed. Only when my soul and spirit were untethered, separated and then correctly reintegrated through quantum entanglement could I gain the ability to dwell in dual realms simultaneously. Previously, I was tethered to the earth realm, and my experience was restricted. Now, my soul is instantly quantum connected to heaven and earth at the same time. That is one example of those new truths and possibilities being unveiled.

The transformation of a tadpole happens in the water. It starts off with a tail and swims happily. Then, it develops legs, and its tail shrinks. It acquires a new respiratory system, allowing it to live both in water and on land, whereas before it could only survive in the water. Now that it is a frog, a whole new horizon of experience has opened up for it. Its transformation has changed it so that it can live in dual realms. That is the transformation in water. The caterpillar, on the other hand, goes through transformation by fire, in the heat of the cocoon.

Examples from scripture

When we look at the Bible, we see numerous instances where individuals faced apparent restrictions that served as catalysts for their transformation and growth. Take Jacob, for example. He found himself under the control of Laban, but learned valuable lessons, including patience. Moses lived as a shepherd in the wilderness. That was not his ultimate destiny. Despite the restrictions he was experiencing, God revealed a remarkable vision to him, calling him into a new role.

David sought refuge in the cave of Abdullah with his mighty men. He, an anointed king, found himself living in a cave. Jeremiah experienced deep anguish of soul, vividly portrayed in the Book of Lamentations. Joseph, in particular, stands out as a testament to how God's plan can be working out behind the scenes. He received a heavenly vision that he would be in a position of authority, yet his path seemed to lead in the opposite direction. He was thrown into a pit, sold into slavery, falsely accused and imprisoned. Even in prison, he faithfully served others, always demonstrating the heart of God and his ability to hear God's voice. Eventually, he was asked to interpret Pharaoh's dream, and within a day, he was appointed as second-in-command in Egypt. It is remarkable how swiftly things can change when we embrace the process.

I cannot say with any certainty what Joseph felt at every stage of his journey. Did he occasionally feel sorry for himself or have moments of doubt? Perhaps. The text does not provide those details. However, when the time came, Joseph was ready. He did not back off just because he was a prisoner, or consider himself unworthy of his new position. He heeded his destiny's call and began fulfilling it. And later, instead of seeking revenge when his family came to him, he showed mercy and grace. Joseph understood that true government and authority are about blessing others, not lording it over them.

Ruth was loyal to her mother-in-law, and when they were both widowed, followed her into a foreign land. There, she gathered leftover grain from fields belonging to Boaz, who turned out to be a kinsman-redeemer and agreed to marry her. Thus she became the great-grandmother of King David.

Esther's preparation involved being exiled, subject to a foreign power, and spending time in a literal soaking room preparing to become one of the king's wives or concubines. At the critical moment, following her destiny, she took the initiative to go in to him ahead of schedule. She was accepted, the king showed her favour and the plot against her people was thwarted.

These stories demonstrate that God's plan might not always align with our ideal scenarios. Who would willingly choose to be thrown into a pit, imprisoned, widowed or exiled? Yet all embraced their changing circumstances and that attitude yielded tremendous growth. I encourage you to view the challenges you face from a heavenly perspective rather than an earthly one. Sometimes we want to escape situations that God is using for our transformation. If we try to prematurely end the process, we miss out on its purpose. Let me clarify that I do not believe God inflicts sickness or abuse on people, but I do believe He uses the opportunities afforded by personal trials to mould us, help us overcome, and foster maturity.

Joseph's preparation began in the pit, and continued through slavery, stewardship, prison and obscurity, until the timing was right. It was only then that his dreams and visions came to fruition. Each of us has a destiny, and if you have not discovered it yet, you can engage with God and ask Him to reveal something that ignites your pursuit of purpose. Most likely, you already sense what draws you in life, as God has planted those passions and desires within you. Pursue them, but be aware that the pursuit itself will involve a time of preparation.

How often do people receive a prophetic word, only to find that its fulfilment does not unfold as they expected? They may encounter unforeseen hardships along the way. The prophetic word is for the future, and we must journey through the preparation to be ready when the time comes. The word serves as an inspiration, motivating us to willingly undergo the necessary process. If we overlook this, we may perceive difficulties as an indication that God's plan has gone awry. We may even question why we ever received the promise in the first place. The reality is that God knows what we need. Whilst He loves us deeply, sometimes we find ourselves caught in pressured situations. And it may be God who is applying the pressure, to reveal what needs to be released.

We can ask Him to lead us into the soaking room by choice, without needing to go through difficult circumstances to get us there. Let us be proactive and pursue it. However, there are no shortcuts to reaching our destination; our continual development towards maturity is integral to the journey. Embrace it and trust that God's timing and plan are perfect.

The soaking room serves as a preparation for us to radiate glory; and I believe it restores harmony, resonance, and balance in our lives. It brings us to a place of equilibrium where we can better understand ourselves, align with God, and connect with creation. When we engage with light, oils, sounds and fragrances, they carry specific frequencies that energise the photons in our DNA. Light possesses the power to energise, release, and bring about change. Light holds immense power, and when we are bathed in its radiance, it has the potential to release, excite, bring resonance, and even drive some things away. This applies not only to frequencies we call 'visible light,' but also to sound and fragrance.

As we are sons of light, we are called to radiate as the light of the world, so we need to be energised with the light of God. Jesus was the light of the world, and told his disciples that they were to be too. We need to shine.

Limitless possibilities

The caterpillar and the tadpole are initially confined to their respective environments until they undergo metamorphosis and can live in new realms. The Father is calling us to embrace temporary restrictions to facilitate transformation, enabling us to experience the freedom of sonship. The possibilities are limitless when we recognise ourselves as the sons of God: such a revelation of our eternal destiny will allow us to live in multidimensional realms beyond our imagination.

However, this will inevitably require participation on our part, some deconstruction, and a change in our thinking. It was not an easy journey for me to transition from linear to nonlinear thinking and actions. I used to operate within the confines of reality, limited by time and space, until God revealed that I need not be subject to linear thinking. Suddenly, a world of possibilities opened up: my capacity for receiving divine revelation experienced exponential growth. Previously, it felt like a heavenly stream flowing into me and out through me every single day. It was truly wonderful. However, now it is as if seven streams have converged to form a powerful river; and I can be present in seven different places simultaneously.

If that seems incredible to you at this point, you can ask God about it for yourself, or just set it aside for now. Yet as John 3:30 states, "He must increase, but I must decrease." This process is akin to the tadpole losing its tail but gaining legs. God is transforming us to be more like Him. He adds to us what resembles Him – enabling us to dwell outside the constraints of the cocoon, to soar like eagles, and engage with heaven freely. We were never meant to continue crawling on the ground and feeding on leaves like caterpillars: our design is to soar and enjoy the sweetness of nectar as butterflies do.

Initially we find ourselves tethered to the earth, but God strips away everything that is not like Him, everything that does not align with the identity for which He created us. I do not desire anything which does not reflect His likeness. I surrender it all to God, offering myself as a living sacrifice every day. I ask Him to do whatever is necessary within me to help me fulfil my destiny. Some days may require significant changes, while others may not. I have learned to embrace even unexpected seasons of transformation, as opposed to resisting them. Continual willingness to surrender is the key: it allows God to work in and through us as He sees fit. We present ourselves to Him so we can be changed and conformed to sonship.

We just give up: it is simple, but it is not easy. If we lay ourselves down on the altar as a living sacrifice, how long will it be before we try to crawl off it again? That is a genuine question. We need to reach a point where we fully commit to surrender, rather than going through the motions. We cannot pretend, neither to God nor to ourselves: it has to be the authentic desire of our hearts.

As for me, I find myself on the altar all the time now. I can be there continually, in a constant state of being a living sacrifice, as I can be in multiple places at once. He is always working on me. Sometimes I am aware of what He is doing, at other times I simply experience the benefits: perhaps my thoughts and feelings have changed, or I notice that I am no longer reacting in the same old ways. It is an ongoing process which I welcome because I desire it. He is my high priest, and I trust Him, more and more.

Soaking

To soak something is to immerse it completely: in a liquid, substance, light, sound, presence or glory. We can think of it as marinating or pickling ourselves in the presence of God. It brings about a change in us as we take on the qualities of what we soak in. Have you ever tasted a gherkin before it is pickled? It tastes like cucumber. I do not really like the taste of cucumber, but I love pickled gherkins because they do not taste like cucumber anymore. They taste like the vinegar and spices they have been pickled in. I love chicken, but I love it even more when it has been marinated in peri-peri sauce. It is still chicken, but the flavour of the chicken is infused with the hot peri-peri. Similarly, when we soak in God's presence, we take on His flavour. We do not lose our identity, but we experience the fullness of His essence that we were always meant to have.

So, imagine yourself immersed, pickled. You come out with a completely different flavour and fragrance. We all carry a fragrance with us, and if we have negative thoughts or attitudes, sometimes it is not very pleasant. But when we soak in the perfume of God's presence, we come out smelling like Him. Baptism in water, in spirit and in fire are other forms of soaking. They signify being immersed in the Father, Son and Holy Spirit. We are baptised into their character, nature, and the reality of who they are, transforming us to align with God's intended pattern for our lives.

The river of life

It is easier to imagine being in water than being in fire, at least for me. But the river of life is not ordinary H_2O; it is the essence of life, encoded with God's vibrational frequencies. It is like music, fragrance and energy.

The river of life is crystal clear. Crystal has significant meaning in the heavenly realm: the throne of God and the foundations of the New Jerusalem are made of crystal, and they carry specific frequencies. The New Age movement has taken these concepts and associated them with pyramid power, whilst dissociating them from the presence of God. Yet such gemstones do contain energy that can affect us: they can drain negative energy from us and even add positive energy. We can use them in a range of different therapies; if we do not know their provenance or history, we can take them into heaven to be cleansed first.

When we are soaking, we are immersed in the essence of God's voice. Even though He may not communicate directly with words, His voice resonates with vibrant energy and life. Sometimes He does speak words to you, causing you to vibrate with their power. Essentially, it is like marinating in the very essence of God's eternal life, which transcends time and space. It is the life God has and wants us to share in: it holds the imprint of the fullness of our identity and calls us back to wholeness and alignment with His eternal pattern. God has always had a vision for us, and as we engage with Him, we begin to see that vision more clearly. This fuels the process of change and prepares us for what lies ahead.

We are going to engage with the frequency of the water in the river of life, immersing ourselves in it to experience its profound effects. All matter possesses frequency, which can also be described as electric current or vibrational energy.

Frequency is the rate at which something vibrates: light and sound waves are familiar examples. Everything, including our bodies, thoughts, and emotions, has its own frequency, and the frequencies we come into contact with affect us. Matching frequencies have very powerful effects. An opera singer's voice that matches the frequency of a glass can cause it to vibrate internally until it breaks apart. Even our thoughts and feelings have vibratory qualities with measurable frequencies. Negative mental states can lower our frequency, whilst positive attitudes of prayer or meditation can raise it.

The principle of entrainment describes the tendency for two oscillating bodies to lock into phase and vibrate in harmony. A substance with a higher frequency tends to raise a lower frequency. Love vibrates at the highest frequency of all and has the ability to bring all the lower frequencies of our physical body, organs, emotions and thoughts into alignment with it. When someone operates from a place of love, it attracts people and has the power to elevate the frequencies of those around them. When we spend time with them, it disarms us and transforms our emotional state. If we feel miserable, it can be hard to escape the influence of other miserable people – "misery loves company" may be a cliché but it is true. On the other hand, being around those who radiate positivity and love makes it almost impossible to stay miserable for long.

When we immerse ourselves in the frequency of God's living dynamic words, our bodies are transformed and become infused with His life, energy and vitality. The river of life pulsates with frequencies that stimulate our DNA, causing it to trigger change and rearrangement. Taking communion operates on the same principle: we absorb the energy of God, which begins to vibrate in us, bringing about transformation and even resequencing our DNA. Through resonance, our frequency is elevated to a higher level, which can activate health and wholeness in each organ of our body. Similarly, it can influence our minds when we align ourselves with it. Agreement holds great power for manifestation. This is why we approach communion with a mindset of agreement, acknowledging that the words spoken are not mere text on a page, but words of life with which we identify. By speaking them in faith, they carry the inherent power of the frequency of God's life, creating an opening or opportunity for us (because an arc always creates a window).

Another example of the application of frequencies in healing is the therapeutic use of essential oils, especially for releasing trauma. Several years ago now, we hosted a seminar by Kari Browning, a former church leader who specialises in releasing trauma through energy and fragrances, using prayer in conjunction with essential oils and the laying on of hands[11]. We learned that the healing capabilities of essential oils can be attributed to the power of frequency. Essential oils are highly concentrated life-force extracts from plants and possess high frequencies. When applied to the human body, either internally or externally, they raise the body's specific frequencies, promoting healing and restoration.

At His birth, Jesus himself received gifts of frankincense and myrrh, which carry specific frequencies, as do their essential oils, together with gold, which is an excellent conductor of energy (that is why the Ark of the Covenant was covered in gold: singing into it would energise it and cause the presence of God to manifest). When Jesus was buried, they prepared His body with specific blends of spices and perfumes. The frequencies of oils and perfumes represent the anointing of the Spirit, and we can also use them to symbolise our co-crucifixion and burial with Him. Isaiah 10:27 tells us that the anointing with oil breaks the yoke (which, in context, was a promise of freedom and restoration).

This is an unfolding revelation from God, and a growing number of people are recognising the potential of such techniques and practices. I believe they serve as a transitional phase until we can fully operate through the power of our words, intentions and thoughts to bring about healing and

---

[11] Recordings of Kari's seminar can be purchased at freedomarc.org/kari

transformation. Since we are currently in transition, it is wise to make use of these methods which God has provided for us.

Flavour, colour, music and movement

The tree of life produces a variety of unfamiliar, wonderful-looking fruits in different colours, with their own frequencies, flavours and fragrances, which purify and prepare us. I have tasted many of these fruits, and they are bursting with energy and life. Taking a bite was an intense experience. Sometimes we may go to the tree of life for healing and the leaves that heal the nations, but there are also scrolls and, in this case, the fruit. You can go and visit the tree of life: its fruit is always in season, and always available to provide what we need.

When sound, colour and movement work together, they have an impact on both natural and spiritual dimensions, opening portals and dimensional gateways. Specific movements of flags and banners can change atmospheres. The power of music is evident in the story of David playing his harp for King Saul to alleviate torment from evil spirits. David's music, which was pure worship of God, raised the frequency of the atmosphere, causing the evil spirits to flee. Different frequencies in music can affect us positively or negatively, soothing our souls and bringing peace or breaking us open.

We can receive healing frequencies through sound tones such as the 528Hz frequency, often known as the "miracle tone." It has healing properties; its resonance can change the physical frequency of our bodies. It is one of the seven solfeggio tones: the others have similar effects, which Michael S. Tyrrell has popularised with his 'Wholetones' music[12]. Crystal singing bowls and tuning forks are often tuned to solfeggio tones.

Some musicians have been retuning their instruments from A=440Hz to A=432Hz or A=444Hz because it changes both the feel and the effect of the music. Our musicians did this one Sunday morning without telling anyone. I am not a musician myself, but I felt the difference and asked them what

---

[12] See www.wholetones.com

they had done. They were playing the same songs, but the music carried a completely different set of frequencies.

We can choose to embrace any or all of these techniques and others to aid our transformation. I encourage you to embrace whatever path God leads you to. Do not do something just because it is trendy or the latest fad: but if you resonate with something, ask Him about incorporating it into your life.

Overshadowing

And all the more believers in the Lord, multitudes of men and women, were constantly added to their number, to such an extent that they even carried the sick out into the streets and laid them on cots and pallets, so that when Peter came by at least his shadow might fall on any one of them (Acts 5:14-15).

To be whole, we need harmony and balance in body, mind, and spirit. Negativity, unhealthy attitudes, and unresolved grief or depression can lower our frequency and make us susceptible to sickness. It is important to take care of all three areas – body, mind, and spirit – for our health and well-being.

I believe that eventually we will connect with and transmit the frequencies of God through our bodies, just as Peter did. His 'shadow' was actually the radiation of a healing energy frequency as he walked past people. Can our bodies radiate that kind of energy? Yes, when we align ourselves with God, He uses that alignment to realign and heal our bodies.

In soaking, we can resonate with higher spiritual frequencies that originate from God's throne and from God Himself. He wants us to align with Him, just as the Spirit of God hovered over the waters in creation, bringing everything back to its original intention. It may be translated as the overshadowing, hovering or brooding of the Spirit, but the root word used there in Genesis is "vibrating" – and it brings about change. When you soak in the soaking room, the power of the Most High will overshadow you and bring about transformation.

There is so much more that I could write about frequency and resonance, and you can search it out for yourself if you wish, but for now it is better to soak and engage with it. Take the opportunity to be prepared for the destiny that is calling you, regardless of the level you may think you are at or what you are going through. This soaking experience can help you to move forward: allow the Holy Spirit to overshadow you and bring transformation and alignment in all areas of your life.

If you know that you have particular physical, mental or emotional issues, come with an expectation that God will meet you in those areas. Come as a living sacrifice, surrender them and be open: allow the anointing, healing balm to affect your entire DNA. Love, joy, peace, praise and thankfulness can all reprogram our DNA with health and wholeness.

Activation #6 Soaking Room

We are going to engage our own spirit and heart, entering the soaking room (which is one of the chambers of our heart), to soak in God's presence.

To stream the audio, scan the QR code or visit the resources page.

> Close your eyes,
> make that choice
> to engage the Father in your spirit,
> and invite His presence to take you
> through the river of life,
> through the garden,
> to the soaking room.

> And by choice, surrender
> your body, soul, mind, emotions, will – everything.
> Make a choice of surrender.
> And let His fragrance come around you;
> let his song sing.

> Let the energy of that river of life begin to energise you.
> As you soak in it,
> let the higher frequencies of those fragrances,
> of the energy of the vibration of the voice of God...

let it cocoon you and surround you in that living water.
Let the crystal nature of that water release energy.

Let the sound and the colour
of the Seven Spirits of God come around you.
Let them envelop you.
Just soak.

Sense there is healing oil,
the balm of heaven, pouring all over you,
beginning to raise the frequency of your body,
of specific organs within your body.
Embrace it.

Be baptised into the Father, into His frequency,
into His fragrance, into the energy of His name.
He starts to call forth your sonship.

Be baptised into Jesus, deeper and deeper
into the very fabric and nature of who He is.
As He reveals the truth, let the truth energise you.
Let the life renew you, refresh you, restore you,
body and soul.

Be baptised into the Spirit, deeper and deeper.
Deep is calling to deep,
with love, and joy, and peace.

As you go to bed tonight, choose to engage again in a specific place you have engaged in the activations so far, whether the garden, dance floor, or soaking room. Give God permission to engage with you there throughout the whole night. While you rest and sleep, your spirit and soul can be actively engaging.

This is a lifestyle, not a one-time experience. Engage this every day and see the life of God surrounding, empowering, and soaking into you. The more you soak, the deeper it penetrates; and the more you are pickled all the way through, reaching into the very depths of your soul, where God desires to go. Deep calls to deep, and He is calling you deeper into Him, so that you can experience Him deeper into you.

9. The Fire of Transformation

So far, in the soaking room, we have experienced the river of life and have been baptised into its waters, embracing its transforming energy and frequency. Like pickled cucumbers, marinated in the presence of God, we have begun taking on His flavour in our lives. However, the soaking room also represents the river of fire.

"Come to Me, all who are weary and heavy-laden, and I will give you rest. Take My yoke upon you and learn from Me, for I am gentle and humble in heart, and you will find rest for your souls. For My yoke is easy, and My burden is light" (Matthew 11:28-30).

In 2010, during a heavenly encounter, Jesus explained this passage to me, a conversation which completely transformed my relationship with Him. This is an invitation to find rest and learn from Jesus, who exemplifies gentleness and humility. Being gentle does not mean being weak or wishy-washy; it means recognising our strength, like a wild stallion with a bit in its mouth surrendered to the rider. God has created us to be powerful, sons made in His image, coheirs in His kingdom. However, we must surrender our own strength and align it with God's purposes. Jesus modelled this surrender by doing only what He saw the Father doing.

Humility involves agreeing with God's assessment of us by accepting His view of us as mighty men and women of valour, enthroned on heavenly mountains, with authority to legislate in His kingdom. Refusing to acknowledge our true identity is a display of pride. True humility says, "I agree with You, Lord. I humble myself under Your mighty hand, and You will exalt me to the place You have called me to." We yield everything to God's purpose, not pursuing our own self-interest.

Taking Jesus' yoke upon us is analogous to a betrothal. It signifies our agreement to be in a relationship with Him, where we commit to join Him in doing only what the Father does. Being yoked to Jesus is what it means to be a disciple, learning from Him and following His way of life. If we do not understand the Hebrew concept of discipleship, we risk missing the connotations of many scriptures. In ancient times, disciples would literally wear the yoke of their rabbi around their neck as they accompanied them. This practice fostered a deep bond of learning and imitation. They would be linked to other disciples in couples and followed the rabbi around like a trail of camels. If you were right behind him, you would be eating his dust as he walked. When Jesus said, "shake the dust off your feet" it had a completely different connotation to what we might assume. He was saying, "When you leave the house, give them everything you have received from me." It was not "Leave in a huff, if they are not interested."

Another aspect of yoking can be seen in training oxen. A young ox would be yoked with an experienced one, teaching it to follow the master's instructions. Sometimes, the young ox would resist, wanting to go its own way. Jesus referred to Paul 'kicking against the goads', a metaphor for resisting discipleship and following the DIY path.

God desires that we live in two realms simultaneously, just as Jesus did, functioning in both earthly and heavenly realms. The purpose of the fire is not to harm us, but to change and transform us: we need to be willing to embrace both the water and the fire. Some of us will experience different processes of transformation. If you go through a water transformation without needing the fire, so much the better. That was not my experience. I had to go through both water and fire, and the fire was instrumental in bringing about transformation in me.

The places of restriction in our lives are where preparation and transformation occur. Sometimes God tells us that in this season everything has to stop: our busyness and constant activity can hinder intimacy with Him. We are so focused on doing, doing, doing that we do not take the time to simply be. It is in those moments of being that God has the opportunity to speak to us, challenge us, and bring about change. We can be so consumed with our activities that we never truly hear God's voice. We may continue doing things because we think we are doing what God wants, but if we take time to listen, He is telling us to stop and move on. Again, it comes back to this question: if our identity is so intertwined with what we do, then if we were to cease our activities, who would we be?

This is something that God wants us to reflect on. Who am I if I am not doing any of the things I believe God wants me to do? Do I still have value and worth? Do I feel the same about myself when I am not actively engaged as when I am doing everything? These are the questions God starts to raise when He places us in restrictive situations or dark clouds. It is in those moments that we have the time to reflect. "Stop all this activity and spend time with Me. Allow that time to change and transform you for the next season, because in that season, you'll need to fly. You'll need to operate in a different realm and do things you've never done before. But if you keep doing what you've always done, you won't be able to."

Sometimes these seasons will feel like a dark night of the soul because they involve intense experiences. That is why many people resist or fight against them: they do not understand what God is seeking to accomplish. They try to escape or avoid the process instead of embracing it. I was like that. I fought it. At least, I certainly tried to for six weeks, and it was a miserable time. I will share more about that later. I counsel you to open your heart and embrace the fire.

When Jesus was twelve, he reached the age of responsibility as a man in Jewish culture. He went to the temple and declared, ""I must be about My Father's business." It was a pivotal moment for Him, as His destiny unfolded before Him. I wonder, how much did He know before that? Luke tells us that He grew in stature both with God and man. There was a process of growth and development. As the Son of God, He had all knowledge; but as the Son of Man, I think He made a deliberate choice to impose certain restrictions on Himself.

Imagine this: He could have been the greatest rabbi in the world at that time. With access to the Father, He possessed wisdom, insight and knowledge that no other rabbi could ever have dreamed of. But He did not go down that path. Instead, He went through a lengthy period of restriction, as an apprentice in His earthly father's business for 18 years.

So I wonder if when He said, "I must be about my Father's business," His Father responded, "All right, but for the next 18 years, you're going to be about your earthly father's business." If so, how did He handle that? I expect He handled it very well. In those 18 years, He probably learned far more than He could have ever learned otherwise. Can you imagine a 12-year-old with such wisdom being accepted into the adult world?

Eventually, at just the right time, the Father unveiled Him and said, "This is my beloved Son, in whom I am well pleased." It was not about any miracles or works He might have done, but only who He was as a Son. The Father affirms each of us in exactly the same way, and on the same basis. It has nothing to do with our actions or accomplishments; it is all about our identity as His sons and daughters.

The river of fire

A river of fire was flowing
And coming out from before Him;
Thousands upon thousands were attending Him,
And myriads upon myriads were standing before Him;
The court sat,
And the books were opened.
(Daniel 7:10).

The river of fire flowing from before God represents His glory and the intensity of His presence. It is similar to the river of life, which is described as rivers of living water, representing the Holy Spirit.

We need to understand what fire does, as distinct from water. If we have the wrong idea, we might resist engaging with the fire because we are afraid of its destructive power. We were taught as children not to put our hands in the fire because it would burn us and cause pain and injury. However, God's fire is different. It does not harm or damage us (though there may be some initial pain). It consumes everything except us, and leaves us as the best version of ourselves, from God's perspective.

It is not actual fire as we know it; it is an intensity of light. God is light. That is one of only three biblical statements that describe Him: God is spirit, God is light, and God is love. Jesus was the light of the world. Light produces heat: if you touch a conventional light bulb, it will be hot. Heat can initiate change and transformation.

We know of different wavelengths of light, such as infrared and ultraviolet, which produce heat and affect us even though we cannot see them. In the process of refining and purifying, God wants to prepare us to face Him directly, to engage in a face-to-face intimate relationship, not just with His presence but with His person. As we embrace the water and the fire, we are preparing ourselves for a profound encounter with God, in which we can truly know Him and be known by Him.

Heat, oxygen and fuel

There are three essential requirements for fire: heat, oxygen, and a fuel source. In the river of fire, God's glory supplies the heat – the presence of God is the scorching heat that ignites the fire. Just as the wind fans a natural fire, the wind of the Spirit provides the oxygen for this fire.

Blacksmiths use bellows to blow air onto the coals to intensify the heat, causing them to glow hot enough to melt metal, allowing them to create useful objects such as horseshoes and tools. In the course of our own lives, we can also go through a similar fashioning process. We may find ourselves in and out of the fire, experiencing challenges and trials. These difficulties can serve as shaping forces, much like the blacksmith's hammer. Once we have become hot enough, we are ready to be moulded and transformed, making us suitable for God's purposes.

Winds of Change is an angel (and an order of angels) that can be involved in helping us through this transformation. I personally experienced the Winds of Change sweeping into my life, bringing me into new seasons, and at times it felt like the cold north wind. Over time, I have begun to develop a heightened sensitivity to these signals: I can sense a chill wind approaching, alerting me that something significant is coming.

God provides the heat and the air, but what is the fuel?

> I feel the heat is rising,
> The flames on the horizon are at my door.
> I'm staring at the ruins,
> The embers of our brokenness, scattered on the floor.
> This fire never sleeps,
> This fire never sleeps.

That was a song we sang quite often during this season in the church here, *Fire Never Sleeps*, by Martin Smith. I sense he was writing from experience. But if the fire is indeed at our door, what shall we do? Open the door and let it in, or call the emergency services? Fight it or embrace it?

This fire never sleeps; it keeps burning incessantly. It is God Himself, a constant presence; though we may not always perceive Him as fire because we would never be able to bear that kind of intensity for long. The following verse speaks of being rescued from the ashes and identifies the furnace as love. "Burn, O my soul!" exclaims the chorus: it is our souls that serve as the fuel for this fire. Fire does not destroy, but it has the power to alter the composition of a substance at a molecular level. This transformation is a change from within.

Just as the river of life flows into our spirits from heaven, so too can the river of fire, purifying the gateways of our souls and consuming the chains that bind us. However, for that to happen we must embrace the flow of this fire rather than avoid it, and allow it to soften the bonds within us. With physical degradation in fire, the chemical bonds break. In the river of fire too, things may seem to fall apart in us before they come together again. The same passage of Hebrews 12 in which God is called a consuming fire also explains that shaking and breaking is necessary, until only the kingdom remains. God shakes us to break and decompose the bonds holding us back, releasing what needs to be let go, including various emotions and thoughts. At first this may seem chaotic and unsettling, but it is part of the journey. As we draw closer to God, we become more attuned to His work in our lives and can cooperate instead of resisting. Rather than seeking relief, we embrace the rising temperature, recognising God is at work.

All this brings about changes within us and exposes the areas that need transformation, so that when the fire comes, that transformation can take place, altering the very substance of our being. Just as wood turns to charcoal when burned, we are changed into a new substance.

Fire is mentioned frequently in scripture, and its source is often God Himself. Leviticus 9:24 tells us that fire came from before the Lord and consumed the burnt offering. In 2 Chronicles 7:1, when Solomon finished praying, fire came down from heaven and consumed the offerings, filling the house with the glory of the Lord. We are the temple of the Holy Spirit, and the fire from heaven, the river of fire, flows into our lives. When we present ourselves as living sacrifices, we undergo a profound change and are filled with glory. Our true identity as sons of God is unveiled, and creation sees it.

In this place of fire, we are being refined and purified, just like precious metals. All the dross rises to the surface, and Jesus, as the refiner, scrapes it off. The goldsmith works with high temperatures, often around 1000°C (over 1800°F); and he continues until he can see the reflection of his own face in the molten metal. Jesus' desire is to see us transformed into reflections of Himself, into our true identity as children of God; and He is watching over us, overseeing the process with love and care.

As we embrace the fire and allow God to work in us, we become vessels that can present offerings to the Lord in righteousness. Our lives become testimonies of His grace and power, reflecting His character and nature. It is through this refining that we are able to fulfil our destiny and outwork the purposes God has for us; though it can be intense and challenging, it is necessary for our growth into maturity. We are called to be willing participants in the crucible, allowing ourselves to be shaped and moulded by the fire of God's presence. We can endure and stand in His presence because He has come to refine us and make us vessels of honour.

So let us welcome the fire and enter the crucible; not resisting it, but embracing the transformation it brings. As we do so, we will experience the pleasure of God's heart and become reflections of His glory. Through the fire we are refined and made into vessels to carry His love and presence to the world.

A dictionary definition of purification includes such concepts as purging, cleansing, clearing, freeing, unburdening, delivering, and providing relief. It involves removing contaminants or undesirable elements and eliminating dirty or harmful substances. This applies to our lives as well. We need to be rid of useless and ungodly things that hinder our growth. Refining is similar in many ways. It means clarifying, cleansing, sifting, filtering, distilling, enhancing, enriching, perfecting, improving, and concentrating. None of this is an easy task: our participation is essential if it is to be effective.

So are we willing to undergo refining and purifying? Are we ready to have all the superfluous elements removed from our lives? Are we willing to be transformed into the image of a child of God, even if that does not align with our current self-perception?

This process requires heat, a crucible, and the blowing of the wind. The fire needs to get hotter for us to enter into glory. To achieve this glory, we must go through the fire of transformation. The entire purpose of this process is to deepen our intimacy with Him. We are being prepared to engage Him face to face. There is nothing to fear; we can embrace it.

Many years ago, I used to sing another song called 'Purify My Heart' without fully grasping its implications. It asked that my heart might be purified like gold and precious silver. It was a beautiful sentiment. But what happens next? The refiner's fire, because my heart's desire is to be holy. Do any of us truly understand the depth of such song lyrics when we sing them? Are we really willing to set our hearts apart for God? Is it genuinely our desire to be holy, knowing what it entails?

If you are reading this today, it is because you have chosen to engage at a deeper level. No one forced you to buy or read this, I hope! You made a conscious decision, perhaps inspired by God's prompting. He wants you to choose to be holy and set apart for Him. You are presenting yourself as an offering, ready to do His will. That is the essence of this.

At the end of the next chapter there will be an activation in which you can choose to engage the river of fire, the altar of fire, or the judgment seat.

10. The Judgment Seat

Are we willing to be living sacrifices? Whatever it takes? I remember saying those words – whatever it takes. "Search my heart, O God, put me on trial. See if there are any hurtful, wicked, idolatrous ways in me." When He did search my heart, I had moments of uncertainty, wondering if I had truly meant what I said or if I regretted uttering those words.

It was not easy, but it was worth it. "You provide the fire; I'll provide the sacrifice," as another song goes. Are we willing to embrace the altar and the fire? Are we willing to endure the heat necessary to refine and purify our hearts? Will we stay in the crucible for as long as it takes to remove all impurities, or will we constantly seek an escape when it gets too hot? Whether the altar, the crucible, or the furnace, it is leading to our transformation into the pure image of how God sees us.

Some of those who have insight will fall, in order to refine, purge and make them pure until the end time; because it is still to come at the appointed time (Daniel 11:35).

Refining is an ongoing process. I believe 'the end time' was the end of the Old Covenant, the period leading up to 70 AD (so 'still to come' when Daniel was prophesying)[13]. So let us focus on the present and embrace the truth that testing is an integral part of this journey, and wholeheartedly embrace it.

"And I will bring the third part through the fire,
Refine them as silver is refined,
And test them as gold is tested.
They will call on My name,
And I will answer them;
I will say, 'They are My people,'
And they will say, 'The Lord is my God.'"
(Zechariah 13:9).

---

[13] You will find a full explanation of how I came to this position in my book *The Eschatology of the Restoration of All Things*.

When we are confronted with increasing levels of darkness that disorient and restrict us, we will embrace God's intention in it rather than fight against it. Every aspect of our journey is leading us towards profound intimacy. The Father aims to free us, aligning our souls and spirits so that we can dwell in dual realms of heaven and earth. These trials are to purify us, to prepare us to encounter the King on a whole new level.

Discipline is not punishment

When we engage face to face, we will see the fire in His eyes. That fire is His profound love for His bride, as a line from yet another song[14] reminds us. It is an expression of His deep, passionate affection for us; it is not a means of punishment. Yes, the writer to the Hebrews tells us that God disciplines those whom He loves; but His discipline is not punishment, it is correction, discipleship, realignment, and chastisement. The Greek word often translated punishment in the New Testament is *kolasis*, derived from a gardening term referring to pruning a plant to increase its fruitfulness. To translate it as 'punishment' is to associate it with negative connotations never intended by the writer. We mistakenly interpret it as retribution that God will inflict upon us. In reality, the root meaning of *kolasis* is restorative, not punitive or retributive. So, when we read 'punishment,' we should understand it as chastisement or correction.

As parents, perhaps we have sometimes punished our children, and for our own benefit, not theirs. Our heavenly Father does correct His children, but always for our benefit and always with love, because love is what motivates everything He does. There is another Greek word, *timeo*, which is used in the New Testament exclusively to describe retributive and vengeful punishment. It is never associated with God; it only pertains to how we humans treat one another. God disciplines us out of love, not because He holds a grudge against us.

---

[14] *We Will Ride* by Andy Park (Vineyard Music Group).

Engaging the Judgment Seat

For no one can lay a foundation other than the one which is laid, which is Jesus Christ. Now if anyone builds on the foundation with gold, silver, precious stones, wood, hay, or straw, each one's work will become evident; for the day will show it because it is to be revealed with fire, and the fire itself will test the quality of each one's work. (1 Corinthians 3:11-13).

The judgment seat represents a place where the consuming fire can consume the wood, hay and stubble. It is the quality of our work that is examined, not the quantity. Nothing good comes from our own self, independent of God. We may need to surrender our self-importance, self-promotion, self-reliance, self-sufficiency, self-belief, self-righteousness, self-help and self-expression. These concepts are all linked to 'self,' and none of them are beneficial, whatever the world may think. The flesh profits nothing.

Here God examines the scroll of our lives and compares it to our scroll of destiny, His perfect thoughts and plans for us. I knew that my life would not match up, but still I was willing to face this judgment. And I now know that we can approach it with confidence and trust, even though it took something of a trick to get me there. I had no idea what was coming, and if I had known in advance, I might not have agreed. It was a divine set-up (and not for the first time).

I described this in the first book of this series, how one day I approached the throne of grace, sat on the Father's lap, and experienced total rest and peace. Then He reminded me that I had personally engaged with all the seven spirits of God but one. Would I like to meet the Spirit of the Fear of the Lord now? In my relaxed state, I casually agreed. The Spirit of the Fear of the Lord appeared, holding a scroll, sealed on both sides, representing my life. Excited by the prospect of finally seeing my scroll of destiny, I got down from God's lap and followed the spirit, hesitating as I faced the opening of a dark cave that looked like a lion's mouth. Was this a mistake? Did I really want to go in there? I was feeling fearful, because my soul was involved. I started to physically shake. I stood there for a while contemplating. But eventually I reasoned with myself that this must be something good.

Despite my apprehension, I pushed onward, feeling the heat increasing. Finally, I turned a corner to behold the consuming fire of God's presence. I felt a mix of fear and the assurance of His love as I acknowledged His worthiness to open the scroll. The seals were broken and the scroll unfolded: my entire life played before my eyes, not focused on 'sins' but to what extent I was aligned with God's purpose.

Now God is so gracious that He first revealed every gold, silver and precious stone moment. He showed me every time that I had been in tune with Him, where I had responded readily; and these came as memories in which I could feel the pleasure of the Father's heart. It prepared me for what was coming: the wood, hay and stubble. All my selfish endeavours were revealed, and all that I had done with mixed or impure motives. This realisation brought regret and sadness, as the fire from His eyes consumed those parts. He showered me with overwhelming love as my scroll was cleansed and those self-centred and misguided actions were wiped away.

I retreated from the chamber and met the Spirit of the Fear of the Lord again. He indicated to me that the scroll was sealed on both sides, so I returned and presented the scroll once more. This time, I saw all the missed opportunities, times when I had failed to pay attention or listen to God. Regret flooded over me for the unrealised potential of my life. Once more, God's love consumed those missed chances.

With my transformed scroll in hand, filled with a sense of renewal and purpose, I found myself somewhere else. I was overcome by a sense of reverence and awe. The Spirit of the Fear of the Lord had taken me to a majestic waterfall. Despite my initial apprehension, I knew that gravity works differently in heaven, so that you can go up waterfalls as well as down, and I mustered the courage to jump off.

As I wondered where the waterfall would take me, I plunged into a pool in the Father's garden, with many other waterfalls cascading into it. I had been in the Father's garden several times, but this was a pool I had never seen before. I let myself sink deeper and deeper, until I came across a chest full of gold coins concealed in the depths. Following my instinct, I ate one of the coins, ingesting the profound revelation God had placed there for me to find at that precise moment in my life.

This encounter at the judgment seat marked a significant turning point in my spiritual journey and brought me to a new level of intimacy with the Father, in which He would reveal Himself to me as never before. I do not know where you are in your journey, or whether you will experience what I did. I will facilitate an activation to open up that possibility, but you may find yourself drawn elsewhere. Go wherever you can go, wherever He will take you and receive what He has prepared for you there.

Activation #7 Judgment Seat

You may want to engage the judgment seat. You may feel you want to go to the altar. You may want to engage in the river of fire. You may want to invite the river of fire into your life.

Any of those things are good.

To stream the audio, scan the QR code or visit the resources page.

Sometimes the fire just looses us from the chains; but we have to be in it for those chains to be burnt through and to break.

> Heaven is open.
> We have an invitation to "come up here."

> Just begin to think about that open door.
> Start to think about, by choice,
> stepping in through the veil into that realm.

JUDGMENT SEAT

Jesus is waiting for us, always at the door.
And as you step into that realm,
feel His welcoming embrace.

I would ask You, Jesus, to take each of us
to the place that You want us to go,
whether that be to the altar
or to the river of fire,
or to the judgment seat.

But take us first to the throne of grace
where we can find the grace and mercy
and help that we need
to go through whatever process You are taking us through,
whatever process of refining and restriction,
the dark cloud...
to bring us into the place of fire.

Let Him pick you up on His lap
and let Him place you
so your head is resting upon His chest.
You can feel the rhythm of His heart,
the warm, comforting presence of His love.
By faith, just allow your spirit to engage.

Stay in that place of rest for as long as you need
to give yourself the courage
to embrace whatever you need to embrace
and to receive the fact that God's love
is His consuming fire.

And if you are willing to embrace the judgment seat,
then just ask the Father for permission
to enter that judgment seat with the scroll of your life.
Or ask Him to give you permission
to go wherever you need to go.

You might feel led to ask Jesus to take you to the altar
to engage the seraphim there,

or to engage the river of fire.
Let that fire just envelop you.

Or to invite the river of fire to come through,
flowing into your soul,
through the gateways of your soul,
purifying, refining, glorifying...

Just be open to wherever it is you feel led to engage.

You may know that there are chains
that are around your soul.
Ask Him to bring that fire
to purify, to refine, to burn through those chains;
to remove all the restrictions
that are controlling you or holding you back,
and to consume all the memories
that are still hurtful or painful,
to let the fire purify your heart.

And when you are ready to go where you need to go,
if you need to go into the judgment seat,
then the Spirit of the Fear of the Lord
is there with your scroll,
so you can receive your scroll.
Let him lead you into that place
where your scroll can be opened
and where the refining fire of His presence and His love
will consume all those things.

Feel free to stay in that place
if God is still doing something with you.

11. Will You Marry Me?

In Him

It is a perfectly expressed love, an extraordinary relationship between Father, Son and Spirit, which He invites us to participate in. It is like a marriage, not just a friendship – but an intimacy that goes beyond our earthly experience of marriage. We are invited to be within Father, Son and Spirit: to be in Him, and He is in us. Love, joy and peace are perfectly expressed there. It is something that can only be experienced.

Similarly, some of our encounters may be emotional, but they go beyond mere human emotions; they touch our very being. When I am there, I am not thinking, "Oh, I feel so loved." I am just immersed in something wonderful that words cannot describe. Everything is created within Him. He created everything so that we and all He created could be included in a relationship with Him.

He associated us in Christ before the fall of the world. Jesus is God's mind made up about us. He always knew in his love that he would present us again face-to-face before him in blameless innocence (Ephesians 1:4 Mirror).

So even before the possibility of something going wrong, He had a plan to make it right through Jesus. He always knew in His love that He would present us before Him in blameless innocence. How many of us feel blameless and innocent? If we are honest, I suspect not many. But that is how He wants us to experience His presence, where nothing can interfere with it or affect how we feel about ourselves and our lives. We are blamelessly innocent in His eyes, and that is a profound revelation of truth that God wants to bring us into.

As Francois du Toit says in his notes on Ephesians 1:4, God found us in Christ before He ever lost us in Adam. From His perspective, we have always been in Him and we will always be in Him. Everything that is created is within Him. I have a question for those who claim that everyone is born separated from God: how can anyone be separated from God who has created everything within Himself? God is both transcendent and immanent: He is transcendent in that He is beyond words and is better experienced than explained, yet at the same time He is immanent in us, choosing to dwell within us and desiring to restore us.

God created man in His image and likeness for relationship; everything is relational with God in the kingdom. If anyone tries to convince you that there are formulaic ways of doing things with God, it is not so. Everything with God is relational, and that means our experience is distinctive for each of us. That is what I love about it because I can engage with heaven and see something astonishing, whilst someone sitting right next to me might experience something equally stunning yet completely different. God is unique in how He interacts with us.

Possibilities

As I was engaging with God while He was renewing my mind and deconstructing my thinking, there were many occasions on which He invited me to walk with Him. I was really excited each time because I knew that whatever I was about to experience would radically change my perception.

"Come, walk with me." We were walking in God's garden, not just the Garden of Eden, but a special place within Eden that holds significance for Him. At times He invites us to join Him there and just be. But this time He showed me a cultivated area, about 20 or 30 yards wide, the most intensely beautiful sight I had ever seen. The flowers, shrubs, and colours were utterly unlike anything I had ever beheld. While I was still marvelling at its beauty, it transformed into something else right before my eyes, equally stunning but completely unlike it was before. And then, as I was still trying to adjust to the change, it instantly transformed again.

I was utterly bewildered, so I looked at Him, and He said, "Let Me show you a glimpse of what I see." In that glimpse, I saw every possibility, every potential option existing in that space, all at once, and God was delighting in each one. I realised that by thinking linearly I had been missing out on so much. God told me He did not create me to think linearly. I asked, "How do I not think linearly? I live in a linear world." Even in heaven, my thoughts seemed to follow a linear pattern. He explained that what we see is just the tip of the iceberg of all that He has created. The possibilities within His creation are infinite, but we tend to focus on the same aspect of the same little thing all the time. God longs to expand our reality[15] and let us see the vastness of His life, so different from the one we are used to. He wants us to see, experience, and engage things as He does. This revelation left me completely blown away.

There are many, many possibilities, because God made us to be creative sons. He has not predestined us to follow some predetermined path: He created us as His children with creativity just like His own. Our sonship is expressed through creativity. But at that stage of my deconstruction, my first instinct was to question, "Among so many possibilities, how do I know which choice is right?" I had been conditioned to believe that there is only one right way and all others are wrong. But God told me, "They are all right, because you are standing here with Me, and you are My son. You can choose from all these possibilities, and they are all right."

It was incredibly liberating because our view of God often restricts us. We think He has only one will, and we are failing if we do not know it or comply with it. We talk about His 'permissive will', as if that is something He will let us get away with even though it is not really what He wants. But He shattered all that reasoning by unveiling the creative nature of sonship in me. He showed me how to create both spiritually and practically, using the conscious power of my mind to shape reality. We all create our own reality with every choice we make; and our interaction means that our choices affect one another's realities: if I had never put this material together, you would not be reading this book today.

---

[15] *Expanding Our Reality* is the title of the sixth event and a possible future book in the *Sons Arise!* series. Event recordings are available at eg.freedomarc.org

Our past conditioning often motivates us to make the same choices, so we get the same results. God is looking to break through that conditioning so that we can be truly creative and start bringing forth realities that do not yet exist. We are made in the image of the Creator, and He inspires and empowers us. He inspired Jesus to heal the sick without giving Him a list of specific instructions on how to do it. Instead, Jesus was motivated by love to heal sick people, and He chose different ways to accomplish it. When I asked Him how He performed certain miracles, He explained that He could have done them in various ways, but He did it the way He chose to do it. That concept was hard for me to comprehend, as I was used to thinking that there was only one correct way to do things.

The truth is that we have the freedom to be creative, just as Jesus was. God encourages us to break free from rigid earthbound thinking and explore the vast possibilities that lie before us. As we tap into the heart of the Creator within us, we can step into a life of boundless creativity and bring about realities that align with His loving intention. It is time to embrace our creative potential and trust that the choices we make can shape a new and beautiful reality for ourselves and for others.

Mindquakes

When I first went to heaven, Jesus used often to ask me what I would like to know. Sometimes I would say something inconsequential and then regret not asking more profound questions. It took me seven years to realise that He was trying to break down certain mindsets and ways of thinking, in order to establish new ones.

Initially, I found it hard to embrace my journey because I could not understand what was happening to me. God did not immediately reveal everything: He was preparing me to accept that I did not necessarily need to know everything (as I thought I did). That deep-seated desire in me for answers, inherent in my redemptive gifting, had led me to make many assumptions and presumptions about God; all of them based on other people's sermons and books and on my own understanding, rather than coming directly from Him.

Encountering God intimately was a challenge that shook all my theological perspectives. I went through what I now call 'mindquakes' that exposed the limitations of my thinking. I was still unwilling to delve deeper into certain subjects because of the complications I realised that would bring. Eventually, God showed me that if I wanted to understand who I am, I had to break free from these restrictions. Saying "yes" to God took time, as I was very hesitant at first. I experienced three weeks of intense head pain, which was not primarily physical but a reflection of my inner struggle. Finally, I surrendered, but I made it clear that I expected Him to show me something real, something tangible, beyond mere intellectual constructs.

Over the next 18 months, my mind continued to quake and I became aware that there were seven pillars supporting the constructs that needed dismantling. At one point, God asked if I wanted Him to remove these pillars, and I said "Yes, what's the quickest way?" He told me that either He could pull the pillars out and let everything collapse or deconstruct it bit by bit. As soon as I heard the idea of pulling the pillars out, I thought, "I will lose my mind." So I asked Him to do it quickly, but one at a time. It was an unsettling but significant time, and now my mind has a different capacity. I can be in multiple realms, and my spirit has been in heaven since 2012, yet continuously connected to this realm.

Every day, I had been engaging with God in that realm while being in my soul. I went through various daily protocols, such as being on the altar and my mountain, engaging with the four faces of God, and more. As I became more involved in the business of heavenly government, it took longer and longer to fulfil all these responsibilities. I found myself longing for more intimate time with God instead of being tied up in my duties for hours. This was when He began to show me that I could learn not to be confined to linear thinking. I could not begin to imagine how, so the Father decided to deconstruct it for me.

Choices

He took me on a walk in my own mind, along dimly-lit paths, and showed me a gulf with doors on the other side. I asked Him to bridge the gulf; we crossed over and stood before a door. As I opened it, I saw infinite possibilities for my next choice. I was in awe, wondering which of them was right, but (as you probably guessed by now) He assured me that all of them were. It was an incredible encounter that expanded my understanding of possibilities.

I came out of that encounter, and I had totally lost track of time. I looked at my watch, and it said 7:45. I was supposed to be meeting Jeremy at the office at 8 o'clock. I was not even dressed yet; I usually get up in the morning and engage with God first before getting ready. This was my first opportunity to choose the reality I wanted. I decided that I would not be late and would reach my office on time at 8 o'clock. So I quickly showered, shaved, and got ready.

When I looked at the kitchen clock, it showed 7:55, but my watch still said 7:45. It is a Citizen Eco-drive, which never stops, so I decided to test this reality. Taking my time, not rushing, I went out to the garden, watered the plants, and fed the fish. When I went back into the house, the clock showed 8:05, but my watch still said 7:45. I was amazed. I told my wife I was going to work, but she reminded me that she needed the car that day. So I had to walk to the Freedom Centre, which would take about 12 minutes at my normal brisk pace.

I strolled along, enjoying the morning and everything around me. When I had covered about three-quarters of the distance, I noticed my watch had started to tick again. I arrived at the office well before 8 o'clock. It turned out that I was in a bubble in which my watch did not match the regular time, but no one else was aware of it. Since then, I have done this on many occasions, getting to places more quickly than logically possible or opening locked gates supernaturally, just by choosing the reality I desire. However, it is not a party trick; I act only in line with my destiny and mandates.

For instance, on one occasion when my flight was delayed, God gave me the opportunity to change the wind direction and reach my destination on time, so I did. But there are times when I get a sense to just allow the situation to play out instead. In Winnipeg, I missed my flight because my baggage was delayed. If I had chosen a reality that my baggage was coming out next, I would never have had the fascinating conversation I did with a scientist seated next to me on the following flight, in which she shared with me her valuable insights into quantum physics and the supernatural realm. I want to be led by the Spirit, not just convenience.

Eternity

He has made everything appropriate in its time. He has also set eternity in their heart... (Ecclesiastes 3:11a).

God created man in His image and likeness to be creative; and with eternity in our hearts, a God-shaped longing for our original identity and where we come from. God desires to release that within us. My heart's desire is to reengage with the fullness of how He created me to be, which draws me to dive deeper into Him and into myself. We all need an eternal relationship with God; not eternal in terms of endless duration, but as the quality of God existing outside of time and space. In the eternal realm, we can engage with Him in the present, which is always 'now'. From the perspective of eternity, our past, present and future are all 'now', and God aligns our present with His eternal desires.

While some people believe that the future already exists, I do not because it would imply a fixed fate. I believe that God's desires for the future is now and already exists, but we, as His sons, have the creative ability to shape it. Our future is not fixed; we participate in co-creating it according to God's original purpose and intention, which inspires us as His children. Rather than viewing the future as something already predetermined, we engage in creating it as co-heirs and co-workers with Him.

The desire for love, joy and peace is a driving force in all our lives, and they can be fully found only in God. To experience this, we need intimacy with Him, and that is an incredible journey that goes far beyond my imagination. In fact, my first book was titled '*My Journey Beyond Beyond*' because in it I describe how God consistently takes me beyond anything I could ever conceive of or think possible. Then He said He wanted to take me not only beyond beyond, but beyond beyond beyond! And He did: transformative experiences so far beyond my grid of reference that I struggle even to begin to describe them. Paul said that some things are inexpressible, but perhaps one day I will find words to communicate these experiences and their profound impact. Until then, I am happy to share what has become my lifestyle, when I feel I have a mandate to do so.

God has always done everything possible to have a people in relationship with Him. His desire for relationship motivates Him; it is an expression of His loving nature towards us. Unfortunately, this truth has been misrepresented over the centuries, and continues to be by sections of the church today, creating a false image of a god we are afraid of or cannot trust. This notion of a harsh, angry, fear-inducing god is a deception that needs to be debunked because the true God wants to reveal Himself as unconditionally loving and compassionate towards us.

"And the one also who had received the one talent came up and said, 'Master, I knew you to be a hard man, reaping where you did not sow and gathering where you scattered no seed. And I was afraid, and went away and hid your talent in the ground. See, you have what is yours.'" (Matthew 25:24-25).

Jesus' parable of the talents represents how some may have such a distorted view of God, thinking of him as a hard, unforgiving master. This untrue perception can lead people to waste their lives, afraid to take action in case they get it wrong. If we recognise this mindset in ourselves, we can have our minds renewed by the truth so that we see God for who He truly is.

Union

Our heart, our soul and our spirit, is the core essence of our being, where we become whole and enter into union with our eternal selves and with God. Restoring our conformed image to align with the sum of His thoughts is a transformative process. As we engage with the heart and mind of God, and with the divine conversation going on around us, in us and through us, these thoughts begin to shape and change us.

The process of becoming one involves unity within ourselves (body, soul and spirit), with God (Father, Son and Holy Spirit), and as a bride, a wife, in a marriage relationship with Him. Psalm 23 was my marriage process: not by just reading it but by living it and engaging it. God was seeking to establish a relationship of pure love and complete trust, looking at me and saying "I want you," and then "You are my treasured possession". He was changing how I thought about myself. I was being prepared as a bride by lying down in green pastures beside quiet waters, having my soul restored and a table set before me. I found it a really wonderful experience, until I had to go into the fire. That was not so pleasant, but it was still part of the same process.

The intimacy of the bride with the groom is announced in Revelation 19:7. The marriage of the Lamb has already come, from God's perspective, and we are called to participate in it. We are not meant to remain a perpetual bride but to grow into being a wife. The bride has the wedding day, but beyond that is the marriage, in which the wife engages in an ongoing relationship with her husband. We are called into that kind of relationship with God, in which we work out our non-independence through intimacy and trust every day of our lives.

Husbands, love your wives, just as Christ also loved the church and gave Himself up for her, so that He might sanctify her, having cleansed her by the washing of water with the word, that He might present to Himself the church in all her glory, having no spot or wrinkle or any such thing; but that she would be holy and blameless (Ephesians 5:25-27).

We, the ekklesia, the gathered people of God, are included in this intimate relationship with Him. Understanding the principles of Hebrew marriage and engaging with it can help us to grasp the deeper level of intimacy God desires with us.

Encounters

Throughout history, God has always walked and talked with people, cultivating a personal relationship with them. Every individual in the past who put their faith in God encountered Him and had a tangible experience with Him. The disciples, for example, met Jesus face to face, experiencing His presence and witnessing His actions; He revealed the nature of the Father to them. Yet modern evangelism often consists in asking people to believe in God through blind faith, expecting them to trust in someone they have never met.

Rather than urging people to 'make a decision for Christ' by praying a generic prayer or responding to an altar call (practices only developed in the 18th and 19th centuries), it is far more effective to lead them to encounter Jesus personally. In the past, the manifest presence of God was so profound that people were moved to tears and genuine transformation occurred without any formal prayers or altar calls. There is no record that Wesley or Whitfield, for example, ever used any such technique; yet under their ministries huge numbers of people met God in His overwhelming presence, which changed their whole lives.

We are learning to focus on facilitating encounters with God, trusting that He will reveal Himself to people without the need for formal prayers or altar calls. These encounters become powerful testimonies of how God touches hearts and changes lives when individuals meet Him face to face. Let me share an example from our therapeutic community, where we could clearly see that one man was carrying deep anger towards God. The community would come to our Sunday meeting, and every week we would invite people to encounter God for themselves. He refused, yet every week God consistently revealed something to him.

Eventually, one Sunday, he reluctantly agreed. Someone from the church guided him to visualise a door, and when he opened it, he saw Jesus with a little girl holding His hand. It turned out that his younger sister had died when he was about 8 years old, and another family member had told him it was because God wanted her more and took her. As a result, he blamed God and had been angry with Him ever since. When he saw this little girl's joy and contentment at being with Jesus, it reframed and transformed his entire perspective.

The beauty of such encounters lies in the fact that God knows exactly what each person needs. Instead of following a formulaic approach like reciting a prayer or insisting on 're-penance', we can trust in God's wisdom to meet people where they are and reveal Himself to them in ways that will profoundly impact their lives.

Divorce

But God demonstrates His own love toward us, in that while we were yet sinners, Christ died for us (Romans 5:8)

Although our relationship with Him has often broken down, God's strong desire for relationship with us endures despite the pain we have caused Him. Humanity has often turned its back on Him, but He continues to pursue restoration and reconciliation in spite of all we have done. Some of us have experienced divorce, which used to carry a heavy stigma (and may still do for some). People will quote from scripture that God hates divorce. That translation is open to argument, but let us ask, why might God hate divorce? Because He has been through it.

And I saw that for all the adulteries of faithless Israel, I had sent her away and given her a writ of divorce, yet her treacherous sister Judah did not fear; but she went and was a harlot also. (Jeremiah 3:8).

He knows the pain and separation of divorce; He identifies with it and does not want any of us to have to go through it. But divorce was still permitted in the Law of Moses; so if we do find ourselves in that situation, He can walk us through it, offering comfort and compassion. However, His desire is for a marriage, not a divorce. He wants to bring us into a marriage relationship with Him.

The first proposal

So let us look at the *Ketubah*, the terms of the marriage. Bible scholars regard the first mention of any subject in scripture as significant because it sets a precedent. When did God first propose? You may have read over it, but it involved a canopy of glory, a covering called the *Huppah*, and a *Ketubah*, a marriage contract. The intended bride were the children of Israel, whom God took out of slavery and wanted to marry. They were supposed to live in a married relationship with Him, in the Promised Land, and the enemy would not have been there. However, they ended up stepping out of where they should have been and found themselves in a very different place.

So it came about on the third day, when it was morning, that there were thunder and lightning flashes and a thick cloud upon the mountain and a very loud trumpet sound, so that all the people who were in the camp trembled. And Moses brought the people out of the camp to meet God, and they stood at the foot of the mountain.

Now Mount Sinai was all in smoke because the Lord descended upon it in fire; and its smoke ascended like the smoke of a furnace, and the whole mountain quaked violently. When the sound of the trumpet grew louder and louder, Moses spoke and God answered him with thunder. (Exodus 19:16-19).

Perhaps all this frightened them because they saw themselves as slaves rather than someone who could become married. A few verses later, God reminded them they were no longer slaves, and began to outline the terms of a *Ketubah*. I am certain that you know them well:

Then God spoke all these words, saying,

"I am the Lord your God, who brought you out of the land of Egypt, out of the house of slavery.

"You shall have no other gods before Me.

"You shall not make for yourself an idol...

"You shall not take the name of the Lord your God in vain...

"Remember the sabbath day, to keep it holy...

"Honour your father and your mother...

"You shall not murder.

"You shall not commit adultery.

"You shall not steal.

"You shall not bear false witness against your neighbour.

"You shall not covet..." (Exodus 20:1-17).

Due to a lack of understanding of context and the idiomatic way in which they were framed, we have completely misinterpreted these terms, treating them as laws, and calling them the 'Ten Commandments'.

All the people perceived the thunder and the lightning flashes and the sound of the trumpet and the mountain smoking; and when the people saw it, they trembled and stood at a distance (Exodus 20:18).

The word thunder in Hebrew is *kole*, and in every other place it occurs in scripture it is translated 'voices' or 'languages'. They were actually hearing the voice of God speaking to them, just like Moses heard the voice of God from the burning bush – it is the same word. The term used for lightning translates literally as 'glorified fire', and all of this was happening while God was speaking to get their attention. He wanted to communicate something significant to them. The *Ketubah* has just been handed down; they are standing there, and the whole mountain covers them in a *huppah*; they look up, and they hear the sound of language and see glorified fire. He is asking, "Will you marry Me?"

The ideal outcome would have been for them to joyfully accept the marriage proposal and become a shining example to the Gentiles, encouraging them to enter into a relationship with God as well. But no, instead they told Moses to speak to God on their behalf because they feared they might die if He spoke to them directly. This misunderstanding and misguided view of God was rooted in their long enslavement under Pharaoh in Egypt: they still saw themselves as unworthy, as slaves, which clouded their perception of God's true nature.

Despite the people's hesitancy and unfaithfulness, God did not give up on them. He longed for a relationship with them, but their faithless actions over multiple generations eventually led to a metaphorical divorce. However, God's plan was not derailed. He called forth a new people, which still included them, and expanded the invitation to all.

On the day of Pentecost, we see a similar manifestation of fire and the voice of God. Tongues of fire and the sound of a mighty, rushing wind marked the beginning of the *ekklesia*, and this time, the people responded differently. They spoke in tongues, representing a spiritual communication from their hearts, saying "Yes" to God's marriage proposal. God then brought them into a new and intimate relationship with Him. Religion has often postponed the full experience of this until the future, particularly the marriage supper of the Lamb. Let us embrace our marriage with God in the present, recognising the opportunity to enter into intimate relationship with Him.

The five stages of Hebrew marriage bring us to this point, where we can engage in a relationship with God that is free from independence and is intimate, in which we experience the fullness of everything God desires for us. To do this, we need to clear up centuries of misunderstanding about the 'Ten Commandments' and put them into their proper context as a *katubah* marriage contract. Thinking of them as laws to be obeyed has led us to develop a wrong perception of God, causing us to be afraid of Him just as the children of Israel were. These were not mere laws; they expressed God's heartfelt desires for His children. If we persist in regarding them as obligations, we will miss the essence of what they are about: expressions of love, blessing, and God's desire to be in a relationship with us.

When producing a *ketubah*, the bride, her father, the groom, and his father would meet under a covering, the first *huppah*, to make an agreement and set the basic boundaries of the marriage. The bride and groom could include anything in the *ketubah* they desired, as long as both parties agreed. That is an important point for us to note: both God and we must agree on the terms. It is not about creating a wish list for Him to fulfil all our selfish desires, but about surrendering our expectations and desires to Him, seeking to walk out our identities and destinies as His children. We also consider what God reveals to us about His love, blessings, and the way He wants to provide for us. We acknowledge His promises and blessings, understanding that they are not our wish list, but God's heartfelt expressions for our lives. In this way, the *ketubah* itself is created in genuine relationship with God; we sit down together and agree, not attempting to manipulate Him into doing things our way, but embracing His loving plan for our lives.

God respects our dignity. He respects His image in us and does not force us to do anything. What He proposes is the opportunity for us to engage in a relationship, not to be subject to another set of rules or slavery. Being a son whilst still retaining a slavery mentality is challenging: I had to get rid of that mentality, and it was not easy. I did not even realise I was thinking like a slave until He showed me that I was.

The law represents a slavery mentality; the truth is what sets us free, not laws and rules that control and restrict us. This was a significant shift for the children of Israel. For instance, when they heard "You shall not steal," they did not see it as a restriction. Instead, it meant no one could take anything from them, as they had experienced in their slavery years. They would not need to steal, because in this relationship God would provide for all their needs. "Seek first the kingdom and His righteousness, and all these things will be added to you" is our *ketubah* responsibility. Putting our destiny in God's kingdom and our sonship first, above all else, is what God asks of us. He wants us to be in a relationship with Him and make Him our first priority so that He can provide all we need to fulfil our destinies.

For those who had known only slavery, God's command to take a day off must have been unexpected. No days off for 430 years, and now He gives them a day off every week. It was not about controlling them into having a day off; it was a reminder that their identity and value did not come from how much they produced. He would love them regardless, and we need to grasp that truth for ourselves. We can easily become performance-oriented and fearful of not being good enough in the sight of God, which will only hinder and restrict us. In God's proposal, He was not setting conditions for acceptance. He already loved them and wanted to marry them. His love is not conditional upon our compliance with rules or legal obligations. Just like proposing to someone you already love, God proposed to them because He already loved them and desired a marriage with them.

His marriage proposal was intended to establish an ongoing loving relationship, and that is what He still wants. He is not trying to make us good through keeping to the rules; we are already good in His sight, made righteous. His goal is to make us free, as a loving relationship is free, and there is freedom in it. Ideally, even as human husbands and wives, we are each free to be ourselves in our marriages, and free to bless each other in ways that could not happen outside of that relationship and commitment.

The purpose of God's proposal was to free the people from slavery and from their restrictive mindsets. He was not listing the stipulations to be met in order for people to be acceptable to Him, as some see the Ten Commandments. Nor are they preconditions for earning a place in heaven in the afterlife;

God already accepts us and is reconciled with us. Marriage is not about what happens when we die; it is about the relationship we can enjoy with Him now and every day.

The threat of hell

God loves us and wants a relationship with us, but He respects our choice. He does not threaten us: He has no interest at all in a relationship based on fear and guilt. His *Ketubah* terms are not laws and rules, nor are they prerequisites for being loved; they confirm that He desires the very best for us.

Relationships are established through love. Boundaries are set within love because love seeks the best for the person without causing harm. The first clause of the *ketubah* is about knowing God and being in a relationship with Him because God wanted to create a culture in which everyone would know Him and be in that relationship with Him. The Messiah was intended to come from this relationship-oriented community. Sadly, when He did come, they rejected Him because they did not recognise God in Him.

God's desire is for us to be an example of relationship with Him to the world, so that others will be drawn to experience that relationship for themselves. It is the way we, believers, have presented the gospel that has led to rejection. The world has rejected us because we have not actually been presenting the true image of God but our own fear-driven image of Him. We have told our neighbours that if they do not accept God, He will punish them forever. That is like a guy saying to a girl, "I love you so much that I want you to marry me. But if you don't, I'm going to shoot you in the head." Would she want to spend the rest of her life with someone as controlling and abusive as that, who would threaten her to get her to marry him?

Our evangelistic approaches have failed to reflect God's true nature. His love has nothing to do with threats or fear. Perfect love casts out fear, so why would we use fear as a tactic to drive people into the kingdom? He wants us to see Him more clearly, so that we can better represent Him to others. Love is to be freely given and received, and that is the kind of relationship God desires with us. To that end, He reaches out to people in various ways, even on their deathbeds, through dreams, visions, and more.

The threat of hell may have convinced some, but they have most likely developed a twisted view of God as a result, and then God has to undo that damage. Whatever method we employ to get people into a relationship with Him, He can reveal Himself and heal any injury caused by those methods, but that is no excuse for us continuing to use them when we know better.

What if we could help the world see God in a different light? What if, as followers of Christ, we were to lift Him up, shining with His light so that the world is drawn to Him? He desires to establish a life with His people that will make the world go "wow" when they see how wonderful that life can be. Whilst the kingdom has advanced in the past 2000 years since Jesus came, and continues to do so daily, how many of the billion or so professing believers genuinely know God personally?

The first words of this *ketubah* consist of four Hebrew letters: *Alef, Nun, Shin*, and *Yod*. In the Hebrew language, letters are like pictures, conveying concepts through symbols. *Alef* represents an ox head, symbolising authority. *Nun* is a fish, signifying multiplication and increase. *Shin* looks like a fence or a hedge, representing protection or boundaries. *Yod* depicts an upraised hand, for praise and submission. When combined, the first word of the marriage contract, *Anochi*, conveys the message "your authority will increase within the hedge of praise and submission".

This is vastly different from a set of commands handed down from on high with a "thou shalt not... or else" approach. It speaks of being in communion with God, prospering, and fulfilling the mandate given to Adam to be fruitful, multiply, fill the earth, subdue and rule – and all this within the context of a loving relationship, not following the tree of the knowledge of good and evil but the Tree of Life. "I am the

Lord your God; have no other gods before me" reflects this sentiment. Who would desire other gods before a God who enables us to thrive within the protection of praise and submission? This sets out what He wants us to encounter and experience in our marriage with Him. He declares, "I am the Lord your God, who chooses to bless you with freedom from slavery, not because of anything you have done, but because I love you. And I want all the people of the world to know that I am a loving God."

Evil and violence

Perhaps it is little wonder that the world struggles with the concept of a loving God when it sees the evil and violence perpetrated by people claiming to follow Him; and not only throughout the history of the past 2000 years, but even in the Bible itself. Much of the Old Testament is written from a Hebrew perspective. When it says that God told them to act in a particular way, it is because that is what they believed Him to be saying, and acted accordingly. So we see whole cities being razed to the ground and all their inhabitants put to the sword: men, women and children. Did God want or command that?

If you insist on reading the Bible as a flat text, as if God dictated it word for word, then you have to both find a plausible explanation for Him decreeing such indiscriminate slaughter and reconcile it with the unconditionally loving Father of Jesus. If the God portrayed in the Old Covenant sometimes appears very different to the God of the New, one reason may be that Israel historically held an undifferentiated view of God and Satan. If we look at Old Testament books in chronological writing order, we see that as time went on they gradually began to view Satan as opposed to God, rather than as a being carrying out His will.

In short, all these biblical accounts were written from the writers' own understanding of events, and are framed within a story-telling convention we may not fully grasp. The original authors never intended them for us, but for another people and nation in a different age.

I struggled with all this too. I have my experience of knowing God; I know that He is a loving God, and everything He does is always motivated by love. I have to trust Him, even when I do not understand. That was what my dark cloud experience was all about – trusting Him when I did not understand, when I had no answers or those I had no longer made sense to me. Would I still trust Him? Honestly, there was a point in time when I said no to that question. I needed to know, and if I did not know, I would not trust Him. My soul was kicking and fighting, and I will go into that in a later chapter.

An environment of love

In proposing to Israel, God was saying "I want you to come back into the fullness of who I always created you to be." I wonder what would happen if we were to create that kind of environment for other people today: an environment of love, where we are all valued and protected within this marvellous relationship with God? What would happen if our life actually became a response to *Anochi*?

That is how the early disciples lived. They knew the love of God, knew Jesus, and Jesus introduced them to the Father. They turned the world upside down, demonstrating the love of God to the poor, the sick, the disadvantaged – rather than just the rich and privileged, who were considered 'blessed by God' in their culture: the rich were celebrated and the poor vilified or ignored. Many parables were a challenge to this common misconception, God wants the *ekklesia* to be authentic, a place of safety, security and love, into which all people can be welcomed.

There is a traditional story about Philip, the evangelist. He lived in a town called Heliopolis, and Caesar built columns there and demanded that everyone walk through them as a way of paying homage to him as a god. Philip refused to do so, and the authorities of the city brought him and his family out to force him to comply. They killed Philip's children one by one, and his wife, and as they died they all pleaded with him not to give in. They understood the importance of a relationship with God and the significance of *ketubah*.

The authorities decided to let Philip live, expecting that he would be tormented by having allowed his family to die. But later, the Roman soldiers involved came back to him and said "If you are so unwilling to compromise, you must serve the one true God. Tell us about Him." And he led them all to Jesus. They said "We took your children away from you, but we would like to be your children now. Can we call you Dad?" A huge revival followed in the city.

If we lived in such intimate relationship with God, the world would see the genuineness of our Christian life. We cannot force people to have a relationship with God; but we can demonstrate something so precious that they want it for themselves. We will gain our authority through being generous, servant-hearted, kind, compassionate, gracious and slow to anger, just as our God is.

God offers this marriage relationship to us. Jesus went to the cross to prepare us; and He was resurrected and came back for us so that we could have a wedding. He invites all of us to go deeper in our relationship; He wants to lead us into the dark cloud to deal with all the mindsets and other obstacles to love that are hidden in our hearts.

Activation #8 Meet the Real God

We are going to go back to the throne of grace again. Allow God to pick you up, place you on His lap and strip away all your wrong perceptions of Him: every mindset you might have which is a twisting of the truth and reality; every theology and doctrine which causes you to struggle with how you perceive Him. Ask Him to show you who He really is, and what He is really like. Let Him answer whatever questions you have.

To stream, scan the QR code or visit the resources page.

So let's take that step of faith.
Step into that realm,
and let Jesus then just take you
to the throne of grace.

Think of the Father seated there.
Think of Him picking you up,
placing you on His lap,
placing you next to His heart
and beginning to reveal Himself to you;
surrounding you in pure love,
pure joy, pure peace;
comforted by the rhythm of His heartbeat.

Ask the Father to reveal the true nature
and the true character of who He is
so that we won't be afraid
of coming into a marriage with Him;
that we won't send someone else instead of us
but we will say "Yes, we will marry You."

Just let Him reveal the very essence of who He is.
Let Him deal with all these paradoxes
and all these issues
by revealing truth.

If we have wrong thinking,
wrong doctrines, wrong theology,
let it be replaced by the true relationship
with the true love of the true living God.

Let the Father reveal that true nature of His love
and the consuming fire of His presence as love,
so that we can really, truly know, in relationship,
the freedom that we have to be His son, to be His child,
and to be willing to go through that process of going
deeper.

Let all the fear that you might have in your heart
be removed,
lying in that place of love and in His heart...

12. Writing Your Ketubah

In this chapter, we are going to consider how to write our own *ketubah* and what we might include in it.

God's promises and purpose

The *ketubah* is about our relationship, which brings us into His promises and purpose as coheirs. So the new covenant is the basis of our *ketubah*, not the old one. We may be using an old covenant example, but one that is a universal principle for engaging relationally with God. On the day of Pentecost, as we have noted, there were tongues of fire and the sound of a mighty, rushing wind; and this time the people said "Yes" to God's marriage proposal. If our *ketubah* is to reflect God's promises and purpose for us, then it needs to be made in light of our destiny scroll that was formed in God's heart and agreed with our spirit in eternity. The more you know of your destiny, the more specific your *ketubah* can be. If you do not yet know anything of your destiny, that is not a problem: you can be nonspecific.

When I first wrote mine, I began from a position of "I want to fulfil all that God has put on my destiny." I intentionally made it very broad and generic. I wanted to be sure it would cover everything I could possibly think of, and beyond. I thought, "I'm going to need to do all this, and all the stuff I don't even know that I'm going to need to do! I need to say that I'll be able to do everything I need to do, whatever it may be, and whether I know it yet or not." You really could not get much broader or less specific. Then I did not revisit it for four years, until I came to teach this topic in 2018, because I had burnt it!

It was burning my *ketubah* that triggered my dark cloud experience. God had shown me that I must not engage with my *ketubah* from a performance-oriented perspective, seeking validation for my soul. And subconsciously, that is likely how I had written it. He led me to envision it differently, as a means to embrace my sonship fully – both in me giving myself to God and God giving Himself to me.

Your eyes have seen my unformed substance;
And in Your book were all written
The days that were ordained for me,
When as yet there was not one of them.
How precious also are Your thoughts to me, O God!
How vast is the sum of them!
(Psalm 139:16-17).

God had complete and profound knowledge of our essence before we were ever formed; in fact, His precious thoughts about us directed the formation of our being. We find our true identity in the progressive revelation of our blueprint, the destiny scroll of our lives. The writer to the Hebrews quotes Jesus as saying:

"Then I said, 'Behold, I have come (it is written of Me in the scroll of the book) to do your will, O God.'" (Hebrews 10:7).

The more we engage with God in intimacy, the more those precious thoughts about us are revealed to us. Whilst we might not grasp each one cognitively, their essence shapes our being and both unveils and affirms our identity in God. So, our authentic identity aligns with this blueprint, evolving daily as we creatively engage with our destiny. This foundation is integral to our existence. This is something that our life is built on, and we produce the *ketubah* from that context. It centres on our expectations of our relationship as revealed by God, in light of our destiny and purpose within that relationship. That may sound overly complicated but it comes down to this: it can only come relationally.

In relationship we will seek first His kingdom and His righteousness, which means as our first love. This is why first love is so important in this journey: engaging God in first love, in our own spirit, opening the door of first love. Remember the church in Ephesus, which was doing so many good things, but had lost its first love. All their activity had become duty or performance-oriented. My *ketubah* is based in love: all I want to do in fulfilling my destiny is because God loves me and I love Him. My love for Him is the primary motivation of everything I want to do now. As His son, I share God's love for creation. And because I love Him, and I am an heir of this creation with Him, it stirs me and stimulates me to see it develop according to His original intent and purpose. My *ketubah* is deeply influenced by my connection to creation, which sparks inspiration through my love relationship with God.

Eventually, when I got through the dark cloud, I really, really knew that even if I never did anything ever again, God would still love me. His love for me is completely unconditional: any action or inaction on my part has no effect on it whatsoever. And I would still love myself. I do not mean that I would love me in all I do or avoid doing, but that I would love myself the way God loves me. Jesus highlighted this when He spoke about loving God with all our heart and strength, and loving our neighbour as ourselves. This is not about what we do; it is about appreciating how God made us.

We are in Him. We are in God's name, His authority, standing within the four faces of God. In Genesis 1:28, the mandate to be fruitful, multiply, and have dominion is central. This realisation forms the foundation of the *ketubah*. In trusting God we surrender to our destiny and purpose. He empowers, protects, and blesses us so that we prosper and thrive; all I have to say is "Here I am". That is my part. And God says, "I have wonderful things in store for you within our relationship. Let's journey together." That is the heart of the *ketubah*.

What to include?

So what do we include in it? Everything that aligns with fulfilling our destiny, guided by God's character, His nature, and His love. We can expect Him to make His abundant resources available to us to fulfil His purpose. If not, we would be left with no choice but to take a DIY approach, trying to do everything in independence. In our relationship with God, through revelation, we know where we can obtain what we need: Ephesians 1:3 speaks of blessings in heavenly places, and since we have been raised up and seated in those heavenly places, all those blessings are within our reach.

Operating beyond the veil is essential and it becomes the cornerstone of our reality. As I say, when I burned my original *ketubah*, I did not revisit it for four years. Then, I realised I still had a digital copy and decided to look through it. I was amazed to find that many of the broad ideas I had jotted down were now integral to my life. My *ketubah*, rather than being an external document, had inwardly motivated me to believe, engage, and live within its context. It had transformed my perspective and become the framework for my life.

I frame my life every day with the favour and blessing of God that I will have all that I need to do everything I am mandated to do. That is my expectation and it is how I live. It works for time, too: I have all the time necessary to do everything God calls me to do. Time is subject to me; I am not subject to time. Initially, when God started to ask me to do more and more, I thought He must be having a laugh. I looked at my diary, and there was not an awful lot of room in there for anything else. But I realised He meant it.

He asked me to meet with people around the world, which meant ten groups of people in different time zones to fit into the diary. Then later on, He said "Here are another twenty groups of people that I want you to meet with." So I had to fit them in the diary too. "Now I want you to go back to meet with all the people you couldn't meet with before." So all that is diarised, but what was I supposed to do with all the other things I was doing before? Well, time is subject to me.

This book is based on teaching I originally did at that time, on one of six different conferences and intensives I needed to prepare. Imagine how much preparation goes into speaking for three full days on a subject like this. I took it to the Father. "So what do you want to do in this intensive?" Normally I would have thought it through and figured it out. Instead, I went to the throne of grace, sat on the Father's lap and said, "There is some grace and mercy that I need, so I'm going to rest here." I rested there for a while and I felt peaceful. I came down off His lap and wrote down all the topics I was going to cover, without any thought. I just wrote them out, mapped out every session, and the titles of the sessions. It was as simple as that. What would have taken me hours and hours of thought took three minutes, because it came flowing out of the heart of God.

At that time, too, I was still putting together the Engaging God programme and teaching it week by week in the church. To compile just one session would probably take me at least two days: meditating on it, getting the scriptures together and writing the PowerPoint slides. Now, I no longer had two days, so I contracted that time into an hour – or that hour expanded into two days, if you look at it from that perspective. I know it is not rationally possible because I know how long it used to take me, but I had enough time to do all that I needed to.

So time now is not my enemy, it is my friend; should I need 28 hours in the day, I can have them because I am not subject to that restriction anymore. I legislate for having all that I need for today, including time to enable me to do everything I am supposed to do. And to have some time off, too, whereas before I was always busy doing something. Now I am never too busy. Busyness is a concept of the mind: "No, I can't do that because I don't have the time." I have the time to do everything, including the time to do gardening, woodworking, watching sport and movies. I have a really enjoyable, full, healthy life.

Sometimes when people hear me speak they say, "Mike, you must be in heaven all the time." Yes, I am in heaven all the time. But I am also here all the time. I just live this way. It is a mindset: I will be able to do everything that I am mandated to do. It would not be fair for God to ask me to do something if I cannot do it, so if He says to do something, I know I can do it. No matter what the obstacles appear to be, they can be overcome, because we have the authority to subdue and rule.

When I first began legislating, my initial inclination was to legislate to eradicate all the difficulties from my life, but I realised that risked depriving me of valuable opportunities for growth and maturity. So I do not set out to legislate for the removal of obstacles; rather, I legislate to be equipped with the wisdom, insight, authority, power, and everything I require to overcome them. At times, I need to seek insight. Yet, more often than not, the insight flows naturally, and the obstacles transform into opportunities for me. It is all about perspective: you can view something as a chore or a duty or seize it as an opportunity; you can reject it as an expectation or embrace it with expectancy. So much of it depends on our attitude.

The framework of my *ketubah* has become intrinsic to how I approach my whole life. Even though I did not consciously engage with it for four years, it had melded into the fabric of my being. The truths it contained had been absorbed within me, profoundly influencing how I was living, empowering me not just to navigate life, but to effectively govern and rule it.

The most important aspect of writing your *ketubah* is to spend time engaging God for it. Ask Him to reveal to you anything He wants you to know about your part in it, but also reveal to you who He is as your Father. Then you can be confident and able to include all the promises that relate to you. We know that the promises of God find their affirmation in Christ – He is the resounding 'Yes.' Our role is to respond with the 'Amen.' You see, God can (and will) affirm His promises all day, but unless we align ourselves with their truth and say 'So be it! I agree', we will not fully reap the benefits. It is about coming into alignment with His divine purpose and plan, which is why the renewal of our mind is so vital. Ultimately, the *ketubah* is about embracing our destiny through surrender.

(You might want to start to think about your vows now too. What is on your heart to say to God? God has already spoken vows that He will express to you. But what do you want to express to Him, considering your *ketubah* and His desire for you as you enter this marriage relationship together? It might seem daunting at first, and you might feel unsure, but just jot down a few heartfelt statements, as if you were penning your vows to your current or intended spouse).

The revelation of God's promises, His blessings, and His empowerment for our success is truly the key here. Writing a *ketubah* is not about concocting a personal wish list; it goes beyond that. If you look at it without the lens of relationship and love, you are in danger of trying to turn it into a tool to manipulate God. But in reality, He is not just saying 'yes' to whatever you add to your list; He is affirming His deep relationship with you. It is all about that relational harmony, where your heart is completely in sync with God's intention. And all of this stems from exploring the extraordinary depths of God's thoughts towards you.

My *ketubah*

My own *ketubah* expectations were quite straightforward: to have everything essential for fulfilling my destiny – what I had seen in dreams and visions, all that God had revealed to me. There were 48 points I laid out, and on top of that, 20 direct dreams, significant moments in which God had unveiled aspects of His future plans for me. These were not just casual wishes; they were things that held deep personal meaning for me because they were part of my very essence and identity. You can imagine that reaching the point of surrendering these dreams was a tough journey, and I will describe how that came about a little later.

Here are just a few of the items that were in my *ketubah*:

- To fulfil my destiny scroll,
- Embracing full health in body, soul, and spirit; and living in rest.
- Knowing God in the fullness of all His names.
- To be able to fulfil those 20 dreams.
- To be transfigured into a fully metamorphosed son of light.
- To be a manifested son of God on the earth.
- To rule as a lord of lords in the Kingdom of God realm and as a king of kings in the Kingdom of Heaven.

- To live in a fulfilled marriage, body, soul and spirit; and to have children and grandchildren who are following their own destinies.
- To fulfil Your desire for me.
- To access the timeline.
- To preside over the courts in the heavenly realms.

I had no idea what 'accessing the timeline' really meant at the time, but now I have done so and I see its importance in terms of the restoration of all things. As for presiding over the courts – bear in mind that at that point, the only court I could even access was the mobile court of accusation. However, I knew that I would need to operate in all the courts, and that according to Zechariah 3:7 a man could have charge of those courts, so I included it even though I had no idea how I might do it. But now I have at least accessed all the courts, even some that I did not even know about back then.

- That I would have all my full faculties restored as intended before the fall of the first creation.
- To ascend the 9 fire stones to full sonship.

I have ascended those stones many times now, in experiences which have totally transformed my life, as I have described elsewhere[16]. When I wrote that line into my *ketubah*, I had only been there once, in 2008, in my first encounter in heaven.

- To operate the trading floors in the heavenly realms.
- To learn how to see things multiplied in that realm and released into this realm.
- To have my DNA restored to its full 12 strands.

All these came out of my own engagements with God. Please do not try to copy (or even rephrase) them to apply to you. You have to make your own *ketubah* – duplicating mine will be of absolutely no value to you whatsoever.

Engage God and release it from your spirit. You can always return to it and revise it when you have more revelation. In

---

[16] See my previous book, *Engaging the Father*, chapter 10.

the beginning I made it as broad as I possibly could. Any inkling of knowledge, revelation or insight I had, I made sure to include it. If I were to put it in writing today, I know there would be plenty more; but now it is a part of me: everything is written on my heart and I come into agreement with it.

To fulfil my destiny, I initially believed I had to enter every single room on the mountain of God and explore each one thoroughly. However, a significant shift occurred when I dealt with my soul, and it turned out that I did not need to do that after all. Back in 2010, I entered what I later learned was the library room of heaven. At the time, I had no idea about its significance. I simply walked in and noticed a book bathed in a radiant light on a small table. Naturally, I was curious, so I picked up the book and started reading it. After a while, I thought there was nothing more to see, so I decided to leave.

It was only later that God revealed the true nature of that place. This room contained every book that had ever existed or would exist, and knowledge that had no earthly counterpart. And He said, "The reason you could only see one book was because if I had shown you all that was here, you would have never, ever come out!" That was how inquisitive I was. Over time, I was able to revisit that room because I had learned to let go of my need to know everything. This experience was an integral part of my journey, as it prepared me to rule over the seven thrones on my personal mountains.

- To call forth the destinies of many sons and daughters.

Again, this was something which I had written into my *ketubah* because God was stirring me.

In 2013, when God asked me to start engaging with people globally, I was dubious at first because I had few connections outside my small local circle. Yet this passion to see people released into their destinies had already taken root in my heart. Jeremy had begun blogging my teaching[17] and I began to receive questions about it. In fact, someone asked if they

---

[17] Our blog is called 'Sons of Issachar' and you can find it at freedomarc.blog

could set up an online forum where members would submit questions for me to answer, and I suggested we call it 'Preparing for Destiny'. It began with around twelve or fourteen people, mostly in the USA, who asked me all kinds of questions, and I answered them. It was great. I really enjoyed doing it and interacting with them.

So when God asked me to reach out, He also showed me that I did have some overseas contacts already. I got in touch with them, and asked, "Who is interested in actually meeting face to face online?" This is long before Zoom, and Skype was not recordable, but Google had something called 'hangouts,' which turned out to be ideal for what we wanted. When I first started, there were two people in Atlanta and one person in Baltimore; we started to meet every week, just chatting online and sharing. They were private, personal conversations, and the majority of my online interactions remain so. Three people – I thought that was enough for me.

Not for God, though. He asked me, "What about people in England? What about all those who came to the Ian Clayton events?" We had hosted Ian in 2011 and 2012, and we had a mailing list of people who had come, so I invited them into a hangout. I think there were 12 who planned to join, but thanks to a catastrophic technology failure, only two of them got into the hangout with me and no one else could. I thought I would see if I could record it because I had never tried that before.

I just shared my journey, my testimony and how I saw in the spirit. Then one of them asked if I could see his angels, and what did they look like? At this point the connection dropped out completely, and to make matters worse, I found I was locked out of my own hangout. But at least it did record properly (though not at the kind of high definition we now take for granted). So I made it an unlisted YouTube video, and sent the twelve people the link. After a while, someone asked if I could make it public, because they thought it would be of benefit to others. When I did, interest just exploded – so many people seemed to be hungry to learn how to see and hear in the spirit[18]. Viewers were watching from all over the world, and many seemed eager to connect with me. So you could say it was a happy accident, but it was God's way of opening the door for me to begin to relate with more and more people. It all came about because part of my *ketubah* was that I would call forth the destiny of many sons and daughters. So although in this realm it was just a line of writing on a page, and I had burnt it, the frequency of those words is still resonating in the heavens and continues to do so.

- To raise up people to take their positions as lords, kings and sons.

That is what I did initially in the original *Sons Arise!* events, and continue to do through this series of books based on them. So the fact you are reading this now is directly aligned to that clause in my *ketubah*.

- To help raise up a Joshua generation and equip the Jesus generation.
- To be part of an Apostolic Resource Centre.
- To know and be fully tutored by the seven spirits of God.
- To tend and cultivate the garden of my heart.
- To fully access the four chambers of my heart.
- To see the Person of God face to face beyond the dark veil.

I had forgotten I had put that in there, but God took me at my word. "If you want to see Me face to face, how about going through this dark cloud to get there?"

- To fully function with the angelic realm.

This is something that has become second nature to me. In particular I relate and interact with my personal angels, the church angels, and the four angels of transformation – and I have discovered that wherever I go, they come to help.

---

[18] Search for *My journey to "See in the spirit"* on YouTube. At the time of writing (October 2023) the video has just reached 60K views.

- To fully engage with the heavenly host.
- To walk in cooperation in relationship with the men in white linen.
- To radiate and manifest the presence of Him who was and is and is to come.
- To live as a speaking creative spirit, calling things forth, using creative thoughts and speech.

That came about as part of renewing my mind. I have learned to live creatively, using my thoughts and words to bring things to life. I did not write 'nonlinear' in my *ketubah*, because I did not have that concept then, but God guided me through breaking free of linear thinking to explore living in dual (and multiple) realms simultaneously.[19]

- To be joined to the Lord and one spirit with Him.
- To be a son of God, a brother of Jesus, a friend of the Holy Spirit.
- To do the greater works of Jesus.
- To create galaxies like Jesus and bring light to the universe.

That came out of me connecting with the universe as I described earlier, and I have indeed birthed a galaxy. I do not often talk or write about it just because I have done it and I know how to do it. I can testify to you that it is possible, but I have more important things on my mind right now, which is actually helping you come into your sonship so that you can do whatever God shows you to do. I am a jack-of-all-trades and a master of very few because He likes to reveal things to me, show me how to do them, help me to teach other people how to do them – and then show me something else.

So although I can do all those things, I rarely do. Mostly I do the very specific things that God calls me to do in my roles as a chancellor and an ambassador. If I prioritise seeking the kingdom and living righteously in love, then I can expect that God will guide, protect, empower, and lead my life.

---

[19] *Living In Dual Realms* was the fourth of the *Sons Arise!* events and the title of a possible future book in this series.

Write your *ketubah*

So let your *ketubah* be a tool to shape your life. That way you will not be controlled by external circumstances but will live with a higher level of authority, flowing from heaven. As we conclude this chapter, I encourage you to spend some time with God. Find a peaceful place, maybe go outside, or whatever works for you. Engage with God and let Him reveal your heart and the intentions of His heart for you. Write your *ketubah*. It does not have to be lengthy; it can be just 20, 10, or even 5 points, as long as it resonates with you and comes from your heart. 'Write the vision and make it plain,' as Habakkuk put it. Sometimes putting your thoughts down on paper helps clarify them, and then it can become a living document that guides your life. Do not worry about getting the phrasing exactly correct; remember, God looks at our hearts, and this is very definitely a heart matter.

You will use what you write in a marriage ceremony later.

13. My Dark Cloud Testimony

I hope you have been able to complete at least a first draft of your *ketubah* and have started to think about your vows. In this chapter I will share more of what resulted from my *ketubah* and the consequent journey God has led me through. This all started between 2010 and 2012, a period that brought significant transformation into my life. In 2012, I taught and published the transformation series, which was a culmination of what I had learned during two years on the pathway of relationship: becoming a living sacrifice and working through the gateways of my body, soul and spirit.

During this time, I discovered that along with relationship there comes a measure of responsibility. God had granted me positions of authority in the heavenly realms, but I reached a limit and began to feel restricted. There was nothing random about all this, and now I can see how everything fit together, though it was not obvious while I was going through it. That was a good thing, because trying to help God's plans along with my own DIY ideas would have been counter-productive.

Rising to the challenge

All of this was preparation for the dark cloud, the covering, which leads to the consummation of relationship with God, so that I could meet Him in person, face to face. I had created my *ketubah*, outlining my 68 points, my dreams, visions and expectations, many of which I have shared with you. Now, though, He started to challenge the motives behind it.

I thought my heart was right, that I was in a good relationship with Him, experiencing daily encounters – surely all was well! At this point my soul and spirit were visiting heaven every day. I was engaging the realm of the Kingdom of God. I was active on mountains, in the courts, even engaging the arc of the presence of God within the Tabernacle, and I was discovering more every day. But I had been praying for God to search me and know my heart, and offering myself as a living sacrifice, so God responded, saying, "Let's get working then."

Using our *ketubah* as a reminder to God of His obligations is not its purpose, and it is not a good idea for any couple to do that in a marriage! Our relationship could easily become performance-oriented, wanting God to do things to affirm us, when in reality we are already affirmed. If we know we are affirmed, then we are free just to be, or to do. But my soul was holding me back from fully embracing this truth. My soul was feeding my identity, and I was not even aware of it.

Every time I entered heaven, my soul would pull me back out, preventing me from staying there. God wanted to give me new revelation, but He could not trust me to handle it without using it to affirm my identity. The *ketubah* was the turning point for me, my trigger. God told me, "You have this agreement for our marriage. Now you're going to have to deal with your independence before we actually get married." I had not realised that I was independent in any aspect of my life.

All we are and all we do flows from a place of relationship. Doing things solely for the sake of having a relationship with God is a dead work, and He does not want that. We cannot earn God's favour and blessings; they are freely given. Trying to earn them puts us in control, and that is what I had unknowingly done.

My *ketubah* was there to help me fulfil my destiny, filled with all my goals and dreams, but God had to work on me. This journey is all about love. I want to give myself to love and be loved, not because I am constantly doing things for God but because He just loves me anyway. It is Who He is. This is where the dark cloud came in, and God led me into it. One Sunday morning, in worship, I found myself in this cloud. I was not exactly frightened, because I knew God was in the midst of it, but I was wondering how to navigate it. This was when one of the angels, Winds of Change, got involved in my life and engineered a season that, if I had known what it entailed, perhaps I would have been less eager to enter into.

As usual, God had been working behind the scenes. May 2011 to May 2012 was my preparation period. You can find plenty of scriptures in the Bible that talk about the dark cloud. For example, when Abraham fell asleep and there was darkness. Deuteronomy also mentions darkness and clouds. There are numerous verses, like Psalm 18:11, which describe darkness as a hiding place with a canopy around it, thick clouds in the sky.

These scriptures indicate that God dwells within a dark cloud for our protection. That is its purpose. If we try to approach without learning to navigate the dark cloud correctly, it can be quite intimidating. He is shielded in it, not hiding from us, but inviting us to seek Him; and we must go through the dark cloud to find Him. At first, I thought I could simply march through it, confident that I could find the way myself. Little did I know what lay ahead!

In May 2011, I wrote in my journal, "Father, how do I meet you in the fire and the smoke?" It just came out without me really thinking about it. God responded, 'You've met with My presence, but you haven't been hungry and thirsty enough to come where I AM within the dark cloud.' I was surprised, because I believed I was really hungry and thirsty (I often have these debates with God – I never win any of them). He pointed out that I had held back, been fearful, and not fully surrendered everything.

My soul reacted: "I'm a living sacrifice! What more do you want?" But God was inciting me deliberately to elicit that reaction from my soul. "If you really want to come, you can. But you'll never be the same." So I was thinking, that's a dare, isn't it? I take that sort of thing seriously. He challenged me, dared me to want to come into the dark cloud. I accepted the challenge and decided I wanted to come. My soul was fully engaged now. He had provoked me into wanting to come into the dark cloud.

I had told Him "I don't want to ever be the same again" before, without fully understanding what that might entail. But now, I really did want to change. So this felt great. I committed to spend time nurturing this desire to enter the dark cloud. I was determined; nothing was going to stop me from coming. It was like a strong inner resolve. I was coming, like it or not. But all this determination was still coming from my soul: I am not proud of it, but it is funny, now that I look back on it.

"You can't continue to act the same way. You must truly want to come; you must need to come. You have too many encumbrances to come. They anchor you to the world. You must be willing to have them dissolved. The way you have been is far too comfortable." Once again, this was an affront to my soul. "I am a pioneer! I'm a forerunner. What do you mean, I'm too comfortable?"

"The gathering angels need to gather from you the things that hold you to the ground and restrict your range of movement. Son, I fear that if you come now, you would not come back. Prepare yourself. Discipline the flesh. Discipline your mind. Surrender your emotions again, and I'll welcome you in to see Me." I wondered however I was going to do all that. After two years of being a living sacrifice, working on all my gateways, doing everything I knew, now He was telling me there was even more to come.

Four months with Me

I then had three consecutive Sunday meetings in which I found myself in the dark cloud during worship. I could see nothing; there was only thick darkness. I felt frustrated but still determined. Then on the fourth Sunday, during worship, I got lost in God's presence on the dance floor, surrounded by swirling colours. It was astonishing. He spoke to me, and said "Come and spend the next four months with Me. Come into the garden, come onto the dance floor, come into the soaking room, come into the bridal chamber. That sounded wonderful! Four months of deep experiences with God! In my excitement, I readily agreed, not fully connecting it to the dark cloud. I thought it was about God coming to earth, which was a thrilling prospect.

"You need to make your marriage contract and take it into the canopy of darkness, into the presence of the Person of God, the consummation." From that I understood that I would need to finish writing my *ketubah* during this period.

He asked me to fast for the final 21 days, and told me that February 20th, 2012, would be my breakthrough day. My expectations were high; I was hungry for more, but still much of it was coming from my soul, not from Him. God was testing the source of my security and identity, which I now see was built on my extraordinary experiences of God, not on God Himself. I was completely blind to that fact, and would have argued very strongly with anyone who suggested such a thing.

Day one, the garden. I got up and sat in my favourite chair, closed my eyes, and saw... nothing. This was unexpected; I was anticipating a deeper revelation of the garden. "Why can't I see? What's going on?" God simply said, "Be still," I had been still for the past fifteen months, but as soon as He said that, suddenly I could not do it. My soul had so many questions, and demanded answers. Why did I need to be still? What was He going to be doing while I was being still? Why had He tricked me into this situation where I was expecting deeper revelation and intimacy, and all I got was darkness?

Over the previous few years, I had learned to let my spirit rule over my soul, at least most of the time, although they were still tethered. But now my soul took over. God effectively removed the power of my spirit to govern my soul, which I thought was completely unfair. "What is the point of being still, if I can't hear anything or see anything?" For that entire first month I asked countless questions and made constant demands of God, utterly frustrated by His silence in the darkness.

Surely the next month would be better? It was not. I knew the Scriptures, like Psalm 46:10, "Be still and know that I am God," or as the Message says, "Step out of the traffic! Take a long, loving look at me, Your High God." I tried, I really did. I looked, but still I could not see or hear anything. I was in a real mess.

TESTIMONY

He who dwells in the shelter of the Most High
Will abide in the shadow of the Almighty.
I will say to the Lord, "My refuge and my fortress,
My God, in whom I trust!"
(Psalm 91:1-2).

Instead, I reacted strongly against the darkness. I was trying to shelter in the shadow of the Almighty, but I could not honestly say, "My refuge and my fortress, my God, in whom I trust." My soul was struggling with that very issue of trust. When I knew everything God was doing, I felt secure in my identity and trust was easy. But in this situation, I questioned everything, and trust was not an option. I needed to know. "I have the redemptive gift of prophet – that is how I am wired. I am supposed to know!" I was shocked at the strength of my soul's reaction.

If this was a test, I failed it miserably. I thought I trusted God, but clearly not at the level He needed. I realised I only trusted Him when I knew what He was doing, which was not really trust at all. When I did not know, I relied on my own understanding. That was when God told me, "I don't need your assistance, just your surrender," which only made me feel terrible. Yet, against all reasonable expectation, I desperately hoped the next month would be different.

It was, only worse. In December 2011, on the dance floor, I was hoping for joy but heard Him say, "Wait." "Why do I need to wait? What am I waiting for? What is this waiting about?" "Those who wait on the Lord will renew their strength." "Oh, yeah?" I felt weak, lost, and helpless. There was no joy in this waiting whatsoever – but there could have been. God gives us His joy so that our joy can be full. But I was not getting any. Could joy be a reality without external circumstances, relying solely on my relationship with God? Not in my experience of this. I would always have contended that joy came from the Lord, but under testing I really questioned that. "See nothing, hear nothing, do nothing – I didn't sign up for this!" This went on for two weeks, but then I gave up. I was at my wits' end, had no more questions, demanded no more answers.

I decided to wait. It was tough, just sitting there in my chair every day, not seeing, hearing, or feeling anything. I attempted to close my eyes and engage my imagination. Nothing. Blackness. I tried everything I could think of. None of it worked because God would not allow it to. I was miserable. It was the worst Christmas of my life, and I must have been the most miserable person for my family to be around because I had no joy, no peace. I was waiting as instructed, but only under obligation. I had given up, and I was annoyed about it.

Then came January, the new year, and I was in the soaking room seeking peace and rest. This time, God simply said, "Rest," so I did not do or even think anything, sometimes even falling asleep during my time with God. It continued for a whole month.

"Come to Me, all who are weary and heavy-laden, and I will give you rest. Take My yoke upon you and learn from Me, for I am gentle and humble in heart, and you will find rest for your souls. For My yoke is easy and My burden is light." (Matthew 11:28-30).

That passage is very familiar to me because of the exposition Jesus had given me of it in heaven, as I mentioned previously. I surrendered and said, "If You say 'rest', then that's what I'll do." It did not make me feel any more restful, but I stopped demanding to know what God was doing.

He was using this time to help my soul recognise my blind-self areas which, by definition, I could not see. He was looking to reveal the source of my identity, strength, and motives. He was testing whether I would take up Jesus' yoke and trust Him, even when it made no sense. It had always been easy to come to Him for rest and comfort, but now, with my senses dulled, I could not see, feel, or hear much. All He was saying was "Rest," so I chose to surrender and rest. "I don't understand. I don't need to understand. I don't care if I ever understand everything ever again. Because I have got to the end of myself. I really don't need to know."

The end of January was approaching, and it was time for the period of fasting and for the bridal chamber. I hoped for something special, but all I heard from Him was, "Wait expectantly." This time I decided not to argue; I would simply wait. I also decided not even to wonder what it was that I was expecting. I was just fasting and waiting.

I thought the 21-day water-only fast would be straightforward enough. After all, I had already done a 40-day fast, so 21 days would be no problem at all. Six days in, I realised I had made a critical error: I had not properly purified the water dispenser I was using, and had poisoned myself with contaminated water.

For 20 years I had been in good health and not been sick at all. I knew how to live in health. But now I was alone in my room and retching violently. Having not eaten for six days, I was already weak, and now I could not even keep water down. My family and friends (at least, those who knew what was happening) urged me to call the doctor, but I stubbornly refused, assuring them I would be fine. Of course, I was far from fine. I was in terrible shape. I was dehydrated, weak and unable to sleep – and those were just the physical issues.

Still I refused to ask God what was going on. I was determined to wait expectantly, even though I was running on empty. I did not follow the sensible advice I would give to anyone else in a similar situation. I did not call the doctor, or the elders, or even put up a fight. I had no strength left to fight, and I reached a point where I just accepted (and even embraced) what was happening. I literally thought, "If I die, I die." I had reached the end of myself. After five or six days, I managed to keep some water down, but it was a severe trial. I was swamped by my emotions. I was confronted with the question of whether I would go through with this when I had no physical strength left.

I realised that I did not know what to do. I had never been through anything like this before, and it caused me to reflect on the depths of Jesus' suffering in the Garden of Gethsemane when He was faced with an even more intense experience and emotional agony, to the point of sweating blood. Despite my physical discomfort, I knew it could not compare to what He went through. He took on all of humanity's negative feelings, our sense of separation, our death and our sin (our lost identity). And I could not even deal with just me.

When He identified with our lostness, Jesus cried out in the opening words of Psalm 22:

My God, my God, why have You forsaken me?
Far from my deliverance are the words of my groaning.
O my God, I cry by day, but You do not answer;
And by night, but I have no rest.
(Psalm 22:1-2).

I do not believe God had actually forsaken Him, any more than He had forsaken David – or me – but I could relate to how Jesus was feeling. I felt distant from any possibility of deliverance, and I was groaning with emotion, crying out without receiving any answers. Day and night, I found no rest, and it seemed like I was living out the words of scripture.

I could not escape the feeling of being alone, abandoned, with no one to help. It was a lonely and difficult time. Why was I feeling this way? I questioned the fairness of it all. My strength had evaporated, and I was physically depleted. I was holding on by a thread, and I started losing mental focus and reasoning. Even praying in tongues became impossible. I was in a sorry state, drowning in despair and self-pity.

That was when I made that symbolic gesture of burning my *ketubah*. It was a way to yield and surrender, to let go of all my expectations. I felt like I was at the end of my strength, waiting without much expectation or hope. I wondered if I would even make it to February 20th, my breakthrough day. Still, I clung to the idea of rejoicing always, even though it felt impossible, and I could not seem to find anything within me to rejoice with.

This was a period of intense shaking and refining in God's consuming fire. It was a revealing time, showing me who I was without God and how often my soul pursued its desire for an independent identity, even while doing what God wanted. I endured nights and days of intense inner fire, feeling like I was burning. I remembered a similar burning experience from my fast in 2010, and I realised that God was doing something profound within me: I was being consumed by His fire. He was testing what would remain. I questioned my value to my family. I even considered making my last will and testament, genuinely believing that no one would truly miss me.

I honestly felt that way; no exaggeration or fabrication. Each of the 68 items that were on my *ketubah* died. I had to surrender them completely. It was not a matter of temporarily placing them on the altar with the intention of picking them up again later: no, they died, and I experienced the emotional grief of their deaths. This was an extreme of grief I had never encountered before. Even when my father passed away, we had never had a close relationship, so I did not feel this level of grief. This was really the first time in my life that I felt I had lost something precious and significant to me.

God took me through each of those 68 points, one by one, and as I burnt my *ketubah*, they died. It was a heartbreaking experience. All those dreams and aspirations were deeply entwined with my soul, and I agonised over each one. The emotional intensity left me feeling bereft. God's question echoed in my mind after each one died: "Do you still love Me?" I could not answer. I did not know. Waves of grief, loss, disappointment, and despair washed over me.

This is not great promotional material, and I know I may not be selling you on this process particularly well, but your experience might be different. You can choose to surrender proactively, which would make the journey much easier. However, I did not know that at the time, and God would not reveal it to me because knowing would have defeated the purpose. He wanted to test my trust in Him, so He kept asking, "Do you trust Me? Do you still love Me?" Still I could not answer.

Would I still love God if none of my dreams were realised, if none of the prophecies ever came to pass, if my destiny remained unfulfilled? Could I still love Him without expecting Him to do anything for me? Or did I only love Him for what I could get from Him? These were questions I could not answer, but I had to face them. Would I still trust God and find joy and peace? Would I have the ability to rejoice and give thanks if God did not bring any of my dreams to fruition? Would He still be a good God if He would allow me to go through this painful experience of letting all this die?

He wanted me to be able to answer from experience, to openly say, "Yes, I love You, and I trust You, even if none of my desires are fulfilled." This is how I came to truly understand God's goodness and realised that what I thought I knew was not grounded in reality. God was searching my heart, revealing the blind-self areas, testing my motives, and refining and purifying my heart. He wanted me to have a pure heart so that I could see Him in a different context and dimension and to take me deeper into His calling. He wanted a face-to-face encounter; but first, He needed to take me through this profound transformation.

For me, this was about dealing with myself (or allowing God to deal with me). The dark cloud covering was where the essence of self was to be yielded and surrendered. I could no longer base my identity on what I did. If I continued seeking affirmation and identity from what I accomplished, I would not be able to engage with anything more that God might reveal or show me. As long as I needed to know things in order to affirm my identity, He could not show me anymore. I would have reached a point where I could progress no further in my spiritual journey.

I reached a critical moment when I yielded and surrendered, and all those things I had been holding onto so tightly finally died. This marked the death of my attempts at self-rule, and with it the control principle that had dominated my life. It was pivotal, a turning point, and everything began to change.

Until that moment, my soul and spirit had been in a constant cycle of stepping into heaven and stepping out again into the earth. I was experiencing unparalleled levels of visions and supernatural encounters, but I was never able to stay in that heavenly realm for extended periods. I was visiting, but not inhabiting. This limitation hindered my effectiveness because I had to try to outwork what I had done in heaven each time I returned to earth. When you can stay in that heavenly realm, you can continually operate and legislate from there to establish things on earth. I had not yet been able to do that.

I also had to let go of my redemptive gift. I had to surrender the knowledge that I was made a certain way, to engage the world in a specific manner. I did not need to know everything anymore. I used to be extremely inquisitive, always pursuing more knowledge. Now I am at peace, content with what I know and only seeking more when I know He is leading me to do so.

Everything that used to provide me with identity and security had to be surrendered. I had been using my soul to engage heaven, so that I could see and know what the Father was doing. There is nothing intrinsically wrong with seeing and knowing but it had become the source of validation of my identity. Whether I knew what the Father was doing or not determined how I felt about myself. Put your own redemptive gift into that equation. If your redemptive gift is ruler, and you can no longer rule, how do you feel about yourself? Who are you then? "When I am ruling. I know I am a ruler" – no. "When I know I am a ruler, then I can rule" – that is the right way round.

I had been using the core essence of who I was redemptively to create my own identity, independently of the spirit. This gave me my security and independence. Even though I did achieve some good things and had fascinating experiences, my identity and security were entirely dependent on my knowledge and accomplishments, such as they were. When things went well, I felt good, but when they did not, I felt terrible. I realised I had to let go of this self-made identity.

"Me, myself, and I" had to surrender, so that my soul and spirit could be separated, and then reintegrated. The separation of my soul and spirit was essential because they were improperly tethered. Their subsequent reintegration would enable me to become whole, with my soul and spirit united and joined to the Lord.

God wants to take all of us through a similar process, but it may not be as intense or dramatic as mine, especially if you are proactive in surrendering. For me, this was a culmination of 15 months of transformation, dealing with the core issue of self-reliance and identity-seeking, and it had to go deep. But depending on your particular redemptive gift, there might still be elements of it for you to surrender and let go. Be prepared to say, "You made me this way, but I will not use it to find my identity. My identity is in You."

God loves us and wants to restore us to our original condition, which is not one of self-reliance but complete reliance on Him. The question was, could God trust me? Previously, the answer was no. After this, He could.

During this time, I was facing a critical question: was it all about me or all about Him? Ultimately, I reached a point where I knew it was all worth it just for a relationship with Him, and nothing else mattered. I did not need to accomplish anything more for God to know He loved me. If He never did another thing for me, I would still love Him. This was a deep, genuine conviction, not a superficial one. I found my confidence in Him, no longer needing to rely on what I knew or my ability to know. On the evening of February 19th, I went to bed, reviewing what God had done, and I fell asleep.

Breakthrough day

On February 20th, my breakthrough day, I awoke completely restored: physically, emotionally and spiritually. My spirit went into heaven with my soul; my soul came back and my spirit stayed there. Yet I felt absolutely whole because my spirit and soul were quantum entangled, as they have been ever since. That is what happened, and I know that it was something God did that would otherwise be impossible: such a profound transformation just does not happen overnight.

He took me to a new level, into the Kingdom of Heaven, a realm I had not been able to enter before. He gave me an orb, a new throne, and access to participate in heavenly courts. I went back to the fire stones, which I had not been permitted to visit since the very first time. Because I no longer needed to know everything, God could now reveal more to me.

After all this, finally I was able to pass through the dark cloud and encounter the Person of God, face to face. I looked into His face, and it was like looking at one facet of a multifaceted diamond. A microsecond, and that was enough to completely transform both my view of Him and my view of myself. That was when I really started to know who God really is, His very character, His nature: He is love. Nothing about this love is performance-based, neither on what I do or even what He does. He is pure, unadulterated love.

That moment opened up a continuing journey in which I am diving ever deeper into God's character as love. It opened up the realm of Eternity for me: I found myself in the heart of God outside of time and space. No doing, only being; immersed in the love and the presence of God. In the dance of the Father, Son and Spirit, in the heart of that life and relationship, I felt overwhelmed with joy, peace and wholeness.

I have become untethered from limitations, free to engage in dual realms of heaven and earth, and even in multiple realms simultaneously. My spirit and soul are quantum entangled, like separated particle pairs instantly connected regardless of distance. What happens to my spirit in heaven instantly resonates with my soul on earth. It is a connection which is beyond the speed of light, which suggests to me that all quantum entanglement operates in the non-physical realm.

While not all my life's issues were immediately resolved, the key surrender had occurred. God then led me through the deconstruction and renewing of my mind, encountering Wisdom and engaging in higher heavenly courts. With the orb I had received, I started to engage and make laws in the Court of the Kings. This was all a result of separating and then reintegrating my soul and spirit.

I was introduced to Wisdom by Jesus, and she led me through various places, the stars, the atmosphere, under the earth and into the trophy room, and even to the realms of the earth in a different dimension. I was able to explore the timeline and see into the ancient past. All this opened up for me now that I was no longer going to use it to affirm my own soul. It was all fascinating, but I felt like it would not have made a great deal of difference to me if I had not experienced it.

As I journeyed with Wisdom, she gave me a seal and a staff. She opened up the 12 chancellors' houses and introduced me to the circle of the deep: all of this intricately connected with the *Sephiroth*, (the Tree of Life) and Metatron's cube. If I had been shown it all before, I would have been overwhelmed. It would have been outside my comfort zone, and I would have been so fascinated by it that I would have had to try to figure it all out. Now I no longer needed to do that and I could simply walk it out with Wisdom. Everything was expanding beyond my imagination, and I felt complete in a way I never had before.

It was at this point that God started opening up opportunities for me to mentor people. Previously, I would have shared my own understanding gained through my own experiences, but now it just began to flow out of me as inspired by heaven.

God's plan is to raise up a united generation empowered by spiritual authority, walking in their inheritance. That is what has inspired me to embark on this journey of mentoring and teaching. God's love is the driving force behind all the changes and transformation we experience. He wants us to be prepared to fulfil our destinies and serve His purposes. This is never meant to condemn but to set apart, purify, and empower us. God wants to bring us all to a place where He can reveal even greater things to us. The question is, can we be trusted with what He desires to give us?

I surrender

Heaven's government is being established on earth, and God is looking for sons and daughters to embrace and participate in it. If we will humble ourselves, He will exalt us: we do not have to scramble over others to climb the ladder because we need to be on top. None of that matters anymore, we just have to be us; free to be who God created us to be, unrestricted by anything that is holding us back and tethering us to this earthbound existence, free to live in the dual realms of heaven and earth and ultimately free to live in all the multidimensional realms of heaven.

I encourage you to embrace your unique journey, whatever that looks like for you. It will not be a carbon copy of mine, but it will lead you to new depths of relationship with God. So please do not read on beyond the end of this chapter just yet. Wait until tomorrow. And tonight, when you go to sleep, go into the place of intimacy – the dance floor, the soaking room, or the garden, wherever you want to go – and ask God to prepare you for tomorrow. If you can, say, "I surrender. Tomorrow, deal with my soul." And then tomorrow, read on and we will see what God does with that.

14. Preparing the soul

Before we can proceed to the separation and reintegration of your soul and spirit, we will need to address any fragmentation within your soul. This fragmentation can result in being divided and unable to align with God's intentions. If you have subconscious parts which are dissociated or emotionally stuck, those parts may be unable to respond.

You will also need to allow His love to penetrate and break down any walls, barriers and partitions you have constructed over time as a means of self-preservation. These defences, which we erect to protect ourselves from harm, can ironically become our prisons, and block the free flow of God's love and presence within us. And if, as many of us have, we have been raised in a religious environment characterised by legalism, such an upbringing can foster fear and misconceptions about God, making it even more essential to dismantle these walls and let God's love and truth flood in.

Our being consists of spirit, soul and body. In an ideal state, these three would operate as a unified whole, reflecting the unity inherent in the relationship between Father, Son and Spirit. This would enable us to perceive ourselves as a singular, cohesive entity, rather than fragmented individuals. Unfortunately, because our soul and spirit have been in competition, this has compromised our awareness of God's presence and activity in our lives.

God's desire is to restore this unity, ensuring that all the gateways within us are open and interconnected, allowing His presence to flow freely from within, just as He designed us. Adam's sin (not sinful behaviours but loss of identity) resulted in mankind's sense of separation from God. Adam and Eve had enjoyed an intimate relationship with Him, free from self-consciousness. Everything they knew about themselves, their physical experiences, and their spiritual lives stemmed from this divine connection. Concepts of identity, worth, security and provision were all derived from God's boundless love, communicated through cardiognosis (intimate, heart-to-heart communion).

In this depth of relationship, God did not need to issue a stream of instructions. Adam and Eve only had to be in His presence for knowledge and wisdom to flow effortlessly. There was no thinking it through, no trying to understand: God walked with them. This underlines the essential beauty of relationships and why God encourages us to cultivate heart-to-heart connections with one another. It is through such connections that we can uplift, encourage, and support each other in our journeys.

However, humanity's history took a drastic turn when Adam and Eve chose independence from God, leading to spiritual separation and the loss of identity through spiritual death. From then on, humanity sought to rediscover its identity from the world rather than through relationship with God. The internal flow was cut off, and we began to look externally. This world-consciousness and independence has been the source of much emotional and psychological damage.

Our self-reliance and the pursuit of self-knowledge have led us to become disconnected from the ultimate truth defined in Jesus the Way, the Truth, and the Life. While the outcomes of this disconnection may feel true and even appear as facts, they do not align with the profound truth that Jesus embodies. This disconnect has resulted in considerable self-inflicted harm caused by our selfishness and self-centeredness.

Overcomers

Once, humanity operated as one heart and one mind, and God recognised that they possessed the potential to accomplish incredible feats. But what did they do? They sought to establish their own name and reputation by constructing a tower to reach heaven by their own DIY effort. Instead of seeking to ascend into heaven in union with God, they aspired to carve out a name for themselves based on their achievements. God's response was not merely to disrupt their languages; He restricted their very understanding and perception of their god-like abilities. This story illustrates a profound lesson. Whenever the motives of our heart are selfish; whenever we rely solely on our own knowledge; whenever we turn aside from God's divine wisdom, we are falsely trading. We are choosing to employ our limited understanding to attain something that God is more than willing to freely give us. This creates damage in our lives, and becomes a source of pain, suffering, and fear.

God's initial purpose for mankind, as established by Him, was to survive and thrive, to multiply and fill the earth. Whilst we have multiplied in numbers, thanks to our God-given survival instincts (intended to empower us to overcome, subdue, and rule over our environment), we have also multiplied in the extent of damage and destruction inflicted upon ourselves and our world. Yet that mandate was never about dominating and ruling over our fellow human beings. Instead, we were meant to exercise dominion over the natural world and the spiritual enemy. Our true calling is not to exert control over others but to cultivate a harmonious coexistence with all creation in which we further its full restoration.

And now humanity is at best surviving, rather than exercising dominion. The whole false concept of the rapture derives from the idea that God will have to come and rescue us because we are not capable of ruling, subduing, overcoming, and being fruitful. We do not need rescue: He has already rescued us through the cross. That act of redemption has granted us victory, enabling us to become overcomers, more than conquerors.

Self

But in our journey through life, many of us have developed a variety of coping mechanisms, defence mechanisms, layers of protection, masks, behaviours, and more. These mechanisms are our attempts to regain what we have lost, but through self-effort. None of these efforts succeed. Instead, they tend leave us damaged, broken, and fragmented. God's desire is to lead us into wholeness, mending the shattered pieces of our lives.

Consider the surfeit of 'self' words that permeate our culture: self-importance, self-promotion, self-control, self-respect, self-esteem, self-worth, self-image, self-reliance, self-sufficiency, self-belief and self-expression, to name but a few. The world is filled with libraries brimming with books by gurus promoting self-help and self-improvement, urging us to rely on ourselves for personal growth. We do not need any of that. Everything we require is found in God, and accessible through our relationship with Him as His children. Put Him first, and everything we need will flow from that connection.

The accumulation of these layers, fragments and coping mechanisms can be attributed to various factors, such as nature, DNA, genetic predispositions, and epigenetic programming. Some aspects of our perception and behaviour are pre-programmed, whilst others are imprinted over time. Interestingly, scientists are increasingly discovering the ability to pass memories across generations, validating the idea that these imprints are not solely based on personal experience but can also be inherited.

Another layer of our makeup is shaped by our environment and our upbringing. Our parents, other significant individuals in our lives, school experiences and a variety of additional external factors contribute to this complex tapestry. Whilst nurture typically occurs gradually, like a constant drip, trauma is more often a sudden occurrence that dramatically shapes our perceptions. When subjected to persistent negativity, or to trauma, individuals can develop thought patterns that lead them to believe lies about themselves. Even though such beliefs are not true, they can become deeply ingrained, entrenched in our neural pathways, forming shortcuts and swift connections to stored memories within our hearts. When triggered, they can propel us down paths of emotional turmoil, leaving us traumatised or debilitated. These damaging imprints operate at a profound level, impacting emotions and behaviours. The good news is that they can be healed and our minds renewed.

Our natural environmental upbringing, or nurture, is a record imprinted in our early years. It encompasses factors such as parental acceptance, affirmation, approval, and perceived security. These elements are vital for nurturing a heart that is secure and resilient. Jesus likened our hearts to soil, describing some as hard and unyielding. Insecure hearts have been damaged and carry a load of memories, like stones, thistles and thorns, which choke out joy and peace, leading to anxieties and worries. Different types of plants thrive in particular soil conditions. Insecure soil provides fertile ground for negative beliefs and emotions to take root, resulting in a life filled with their fruit.

Curses, vows, agreements and lies may also contribute to this complex trail of damage, shaping our understanding of ourselves and the world around us. When I vowed never to be hurt again, as I described in chapter 3, it totally shut down my emotions. Before that, I used to experience very normal emotions; afterwards I was like a block of granite – at least on the surface. People's words and actions seemed to slip past me with no effect whatsoever. Deep inside, though, I was hurting. It was not until I reconnected with my emotions as I engaged with God that I recognised the turmoil going on within me.

Our nature is complex, seeded as it is with the imprints of family records and behaviours passed down as iniquity. It includes a range of genetic factors and predispositions. If nurture is the record of our early years, then trauma is the record of our experiences. Whether abuse (physical, sexual, emotional, psychological or verbal) or the result of various incidents and accidents, these can be etched within the cells of our bodies, giving rise to fear, grief, loss and anxiety. Even seemingly mundane life events like moving home during childhood can be traumatic and lead to identity crises.

For the word of God is living and active and sharper than any two-edged sword, and piercing as far as the division of soul and spirit, of both joints and marrow, and able to judge the thoughts and intentions of the heart (Hebrews 4:12).

The writer to the Hebrews mentions dividing, separating, and judging; dividing between soul and spirit as between bone and marrow. These layers can encompass a range of behaviours, thoughts, intentions, and motives; and their root or source, whether it be genetic transgression, sin or iniquity. They collectively shape who we are, and addressing them involves three distinct levels of transformation.

Many inner healing and deliverance methods focus primarily on addressing behaviours, seeking to reveal why individuals think and act the way they do. However, when we engage with the realms of the kingdom, we need to go beyond surface-level healing. It is not that we ignore the behaviours, but it is imperative to delve into the motives of our hearts that have fuelled those behaviours. We need pure hearts if we are going to function in sonship.

Surface-level healing, which deals with coping mechanisms and skins, can bring us as far as the Kingdom of God realm and allow us to operate as lords, from a heavenly perspective. However, God's desire is not merely for us to stay there but to mature into kingship. Engaging in kingship necessitates going deeper and dealing with the motives of our hearts. I found dealing with the motives of my heart extremely unpleasant and distasteful to my soul. It required confronting the truth about myself, even when that truth was unpalatable. God wanted to purify my motives, so that I would no longer rely on (nor need to constantly battle against) negative aspects of my nature. The power of the body and blood of Jesus in communion is an effective method of dealing with the motives of our heart.

There exists also a deeper level, the order of Melchizedek, which has no earthly genealogy and so is not part of Adam's lineage. As new creations in Christ, we can embrace a heavenly lineage and operate as kings and priests in this new order.

If we want to come into true sonship, we need some genetic transformation, under God's guidance. It is essential not to dig into this on our own but to surrender ourselves as living sacrifices, allowing Him to work in us as He sees fit. Rest in Him: do not rush ahead in your own strength.

Blessed be the God and Father of our Lord Jesus Christ, who has blessed us with every spiritual blessing in the heavenly places in Christ, just as He chose us in Him before the foundation of the world, that we would be holy and blameless before Him. In love He predestined us to adoption as sons through Jesus Christ to Himself, according to the kind intention of His will, to the praise of the glory of His grace, which He freely bestowed on us in the Beloved (Ephesians 1:3-6).

In the Mirror Bible, Francois Du Toit expresses it this way:

He associated us in Christ before the fall of the world. Jesus is God's mind made up about us. He always knew in his love that he would present us again face to face before him in blameless innocence. He is the architect of our design, his heart dream realized our coming of age in Christ (Ephesians 1:4-5 Mirror).

Wholeness is not just possible; it is our destiny to be whole, united as one, and embraced as sons and daughters of God. The kind intention of His will: that is what He is like. Everything about Him is kind and good, and He wants us to know Him in that way because we have been adopted into His family as His sons and daughters.

Reset

Now may the God of peace Himself sanctify you entirely; and may your spirit and soul and body be preserved complete, without blame at the coming of our Lord Jesus Christ (1 Thessalonians 5:23).

As we have seen before, 'at the coming' is a poor translation of *en ho parousia*. It is used because the translators typically believe in a future 'Second Coming' of Christ, and assume that this alludes to it. Remove that expectation and you are free to translate it as what it really says, 'in the presence.' There is no need to put off sanctification and unification to a future time.

There, away from any effort of your own, discover how the God of perfect peace, who fused you skillfully into oneness – just like a master craftsman would dovetail a carpentry joint – has personally perfected and sanctified the entire harmony of your being without your help. He has restored the detailed default settings. You were re-booted to fully participate in the life of your design, in your spirit, soul and body in blameless innocence in the immediate presence of our Lord Jesus Christ. (It is not in my "I-used-to-be-ness" or "I'm-trying-to-become-ness", but in my "I-am-ness." The word *eirene*, translated peace, refers to the dovetail joint in carpentry. The word *parousia*, suggests immediate presence...) (1 Thessalonians 5:23 Mirror, with the translator's note).

It is not dependent on our efforts; it is about allowing the God of perfect peace to do His work. Our cooperation can facilitate the process, but as God told me, "I don't need your assistance; just your surrender." Jesus is in the Father, the Father is in Him; I am in Him, and He is in me. That reality begins to transform and shape us so that this oneness can be our lived reality – whole, complete, and utterly one.

The power of the cross

Jesus fully identified with our humanity as the Son of Man and completely understood our brokenness. Even when He cried out on the cross, "My God, my God, why have you forsaken me?" God had not forsaken Him[20]. The Father and the Spirit were within Him, and He in them. Even amidst the turmoil, the cloud of God's presence enveloped Him: this same dark cloud. It was not a cloud of demons, as some imagine, but God's presence surrounding the cross.

Therefore, since the children share in flesh and blood, He Himself likewise also partook of the same, that through death

---

[20] Jesus was quoting Psalm 22. In that society, when a rabbi quoted the opening verse, his hearers would know that he was referencing the whole psalm, and would know what else it said. If you read the whole psalm, you will see that God had not forsaken the psalmist, but responded to his groaning. God did not forsake Jesus either.

He might render powerless him who had the power of death, that is, the devil, and might free those who were through fear of death subject to slavery all their lives (Hebrews 2:14-15).

For we do not have a high priest who cannot sympathize with our weaknesses, but One who has been tempted in all things just as we are, yet without sin. Therefore let us draw near with confidence to the throne of grace, so that we may receive mercy and find grace to help in time of need (Hebrews 4:15-16).

The power of the cross lies in the fact that Jesus came to represent fallen Adam, not sinless Adam. He fully identified with us in order to free us from slavery to sin and death. He remained sinless because He never lost His divine image. Jesus was crying my cry because He was representing me in my spiritual death; and now He is representing me in my resurrection. We were co-crucified with Him; we went into the grave; we were dead and buried. We were resurrected and ascended, and raised up to be seated in heavenly places. The whole package belongs to us as God's children.

No fear

"Son, the goal of wholeness is the restoration of all that has been lost, broken, fragmented and fractured. All that has been used to protect can be removed. The coping and defence mechanisms that have been employed by the subconscious mind can be safely removed in My presence."

We can confidently approach the throne of grace without needing to hide anything from God, because He knows us intimately and loves us unconditionally. We do not need to guard ourselves against Him. The safe removal of these protective hindrances will allow us to rest in and enjoy the fullness of His presence, free from barriers, walls, partitions or any kind of separation, real or imagined. It is a state of being where He is fully within us, and we are fully in Him.

There is no fear in love; but perfect love casts out fear because fear involves punishment, and the one who fears is not perfected in love (1 John 4:18).

In His presence there is no fear but instead an abundance of joy and peace beyond earthly understanding. John's assertion here implies that if you are apprehensive about being punished by God, it is because you have not yet grasped His love. Those who perceive God as a punishing deity and who propagate this image are sadly unaware of His perfect love – and are hindering the world from experiencing it. Jesus embodies this perfect love. He is the perfect manifestation of God's perfect love: God is love and He wants us to know it.

Jesus told His disciples:

"Peace be with you. I give you my own peace – this is not the kind the world gives – this is peace in the midst of troubled times; therefore you have nothing to fear. Let not your hearts be timid." (John 14:27 Mirror).

Yet many of us experience troubled and fearful hearts due to what goes on inside us. Jesus offers His peace, a unique peace that prevails even in turbulent times, so we have no reason to fear; our hearts need not be timid.

Whoever resonates and treasures the completeness of my prophetic purpose cannot but fall in love with me and also find themselves to be fully participating in my Father's love and I will love this one and make myself distinctly known and real to each one individually. In this embrace of inseparable union, love rules. (Intimacy is not the result of suspicious scrutiny but the inevitable fruit of trust.) (John 14:21 Mirror, with translator's note).

This underscores the significance of relationships and reflects Jesus' longing for us to be one, as we can read in John 17. Whether individually or collectively, the goal is unity, an inseparable and intimate oneness. As Francois Du Toit explains:

> Note that it is not our knowing that positions Jesus in the Father, or us in them, or the Spirit of Christ in us. Our knowing simply awakens us to the reality of our redeemed

union. Gold does not become gold when it is discovered, but it certainly becomes currency[21].

The truth is and remains the truth whether we know it or not. Our knowing simply allows us to live in it, to participate in the divine plan. The repercussions of this will undermine one of the major tenets of modern evangelicalism, because the 'all' who died in Adam are the same 'all' who are now made alive in Christ. All have been included. The Holy Spirit has been poured out on all flesh. All have been born from above. None of this is contingent upon our altar calls, sinners' prayers or decisions for Christ. It is all the result of what He has accomplished. He has reconciled the entire creation to Himself, not counting their sins against them.

That is the gospel, the real good news, the message of love and inclusion, not that people are separated from God because of their sins and must express sorrow and ask forgiveness before God can love them. Sadly, it is not the message that most of the church chooses to preach. How can we expect people to embrace a wonderful, loving God who will torment them eternally unless they believe? He does not, and He will not. He loves everyone and is actively at work in every individual whether they are aware of it or not. Let us stop telling people that they are separated from God, that He despises (and cannot even look at) their sin. Instead, let our preaching reveal that God is already at work within them.

Consider Saul's transformational experience in his encounter on the road to Damascus. A blinding light enveloped him. Interestingly, when he writes about this in Galatians 1:16 he does not say that God revealed Himself in the light; rather, that the Father revealed Jesus in him (Saul). This distinction is critical. The Father had always been at work within him, and was now revealing Jesus in him. Later, he related the story to King Agrippa:

---

[21] Francois Du Toit, notes on John 14:20 in the Mirror Bible.

"While so engaged as I was journeying to Damascus with the authority and commission of the chief priests, at midday, O King, I saw on the way a light from heaven, brighter than the sun, shining all around me and those who were journeying with me. And when we had all fallen to the ground, I heard a voice saying to me in the Hebrew dialect, 'Saul, Saul, why are you persecuting Me? It is hard for you to kick against the goads.' And I said, 'Who are You, Lord?' And the Lord said, 'I am Jesus whom you are persecuting'" (Acts 26:12-15).

Paul's encounter led him to ask, "Who are you, Lord?" And the response he received was, "I am Jesus, the One you've been persecuting. You've been resisting My work in you, resisting My efforts to lead you to abandon self-righteousness and embrace My love."

This revelation was so profound that Paul retreated to the desert for years, as it completely upended everything he had ever believed. He had to undergo a profound mind renewal in intimacy with God over several years, because his previous mindset was so deeply ingrained. He was a Pharisee of Pharisees, a Hebrew of Hebrews, a distinguished scholar; and he thought he had the inside track with God. God, through His love, radically transformed him, making him an advocate of inclusion.

I know these are challenging concepts, and there will be many more to come if you continue on this journey. Yet you will resonate with the love of God. Your soul might be challenged by it, and your mind might be offended by it, and any religious spirits operating will definitely be stirred up by it, but your own spirit will relate to it. You have been in the heart of God; you were birthed out of the heart of God; your spirit has memory of the heart of God. It is just that you have been disconnected from it and God wants to reconnect you so that you know who you are from an eternal perspective.

Strongholds

Are we willing to allow the love of God to penetrate these barriers, walls and separations we have built within ourselves and wash away all these things that hold us captive? Consider what might need addressing within our soul (or some may call it our subconscious mind or heart). Our soul is complex. It is where our memories, beliefs and values, true or false, reside. It is also where our mindsets form. The brain is not the place where all this is formulated or stored; rather, it is our heart that holds these memories and records. Our brain serves as the pathway that connects to our heart; and our heart shows significantly more electromagnetic activity than our brain.

When our hearts hold memories of pain, damage, rejection or lies, we create defence mechanisms and behavioural patterns to shield ourselves from further harm. We fortify our minds with strongholds, creating mental barriers to protect ourselves. We may seek to deter people from getting too close, pushing them away out of fear of more hurt or damage. Familiar spirits may feed these negative thoughts, constantly reminding us of our hurts and failures.

All these inner dynamics, rooted in the heart, feed into our conscious or subconscious mind. They influence our thoughts, behaviours, attitudes and emotions, causing doubts, fears and insecurities to surface. It is a continuous cycle of triggering and loading, just as a program in a computer's hard drive is launched by clicking an icon on the screen. Sometimes we can find ourselves overwhelmed, like a computer with too much data and no free space on its drive, constantly churning thoughts.

Anyone who embarks on this contemplative journey quickly discovers how challenging it can be. When you sit down to meditate or pray, attempting to quiet your mind can lead to an avalanche of thoughts, ranging from mundane tasks like needing to buy groceries to deeper questions of existence. Such thoughts can be triggered by a variety of factors, including environmental cues, fears, and life experiences. The key is to find God in the midst of this mental chaos. Placing Him on the throne of our lives is essential because if He is not ruling over our lives, then our soul will. And when we are in charge, we will use all these mental processes to avoid tackling the issues. However, when we invite God to assume His rightful place on the throne, He starts addressing and healing them.

To renew our minds and uncover the truth, we need revelation. This truth is not merely a concept, ideal, theology or doctrine: Jesus is the living Word of God, and Truth itself. Engaging with this Truth will reveal and eliminate the lies ingrained within us. Knowing God as love and allowing Him to work in our hearts will see all our defence mechanisms dismantled.

Emotions

Emotions are closely tied to our thoughts and hearts. Emotions encompass feelings of self-worth, esteem, love, security, acceptance, and value – essential needs that God designed to be fulfilled in Him. If we seek to get these needs met elsewhere, it can lead to co-dependent relationships and a range of damaging emotions such as insecurity, disappointment, rejection, guilt, despondency, resentment, bitterness and shame. These create a complex web of emotions and thoughts that govern our behaviours, attitudes and reactions. Toxic thinking and toxic emotions are a powerful mixture that produces a toxic life. If I am painting a really extreme picture, all of us can relate to it in some degree. As psychologist John Seymour[22] has said, "Emotions make excellent servants, but tyrannical masters."

God's desire is to bring healing to our lives, but that can only happen as we surrender the throne of our government and our souls to Him. When He takes His place within us, He provides all the esteem, love, worth, security and value we desperately need, reshaping our motivations, empowering and enabling us to operate with a transformed mindset.

---

[22] John Seymour, in *Introducing Neuro-Linguistic Programming: Psychological Skills for Understanding and Influencing People* by Joseph O'Connor and John Seymour, Thorsons, 1990.

Finally, we come to our will. This is where the principle of sin resides: iniquity, stubbornness, rebellion, doubt, fear and control. Historically we may have used even these attributes to safeguard ourselves. However, as we allow Jesus and the Father to take their rightful place on the throne of our lives, we surrender our will.

As our minds undergo transformation, a new way of thinking emerges. We worship and surrender to God, who begins to fill us with an array of positive attributes: confidence, humility, endurance, boldness, courage, patience, perseverance and self-control. These begin to shape us from within. To heal and grow, we must first understand who we were created to be, and align ourselves with that divine purpose.

One significant problem we encounter is trauma. Trauma has the power to create instant neural pathways to memories that can continue to influence us even years after we have totally forgotten the incident, or cause dissociation by completely bypassing our memory of the traumatic event. That is what happened to me, as I described in chapter 2. Sometimes, we simply do not know why we behave in certain ways, and our entire lives may be impacted by such hidden trauma. It comes in many forms, and what adversely affects one person may have minimal impact on another. It is a deeply subjective experience, making it almost impossible for anyone else to determine what may be 'wrong' with you. A person who has been raised in a secure family environment who experiences a particular event may find it has little effect because they know they are loved and accepted. On the other hand, the same event could be life-altering and devastating for another individual. The damage done by trauma is not necessarily due to its severity, but to its impact. What might seem trivial to one person can be profoundly damaging for another.

Dissociation is not exclusive to extreme cases like physical or sexual abuse. I did not experience either, yet I still dissociated because of the damage caused by fear. Each of us has unique triggers and experiences, but the key is that God desires to restore us and make us whole.

We may have emotionally stuck parts within us. Have you ever said something to someone that triggered an emotional reaction seemingly out of all proportion to the situation? They might suddenly act like a 5-year-old, or a petulant teenager, leaving you wondering, "What did I say?" These reactions are often beyond their control because they are stuck emotionally at a particular age. These are not necessarily full-blown dissociative personalities, but rather emotionally charged areas that become agitated in certain circumstances. God can show us where we might be stuck at a certain age emotionally. We can then welcome that younger part of ourselves to embrace the love of Jesus and be set free. Sometimes, this process might involve uncovering specific memories and offering forgiveness to those involved, but often God can immediately heal these areas as we seek Him.

Trauma can leave deep imprints not just in our minds and emotions, but in the very cells of our physical body. To truly heal and become whole, this trauma needs to be released from every part of our being – our cells, emotions, heart and mind. The stored memories can be released and healed. We can invite Jesus, the Prince of Peace and the embodiment of perfect love, into these areas of fear, allowing Him to bring healing. It is our choice. We can choose to hold onto these traumas, or we can choose to open ourselves to God, lowering the barriers and disengaging the protection mechanisms so that He can come in and heal the trauma within us and bring us into wholeness.

Declaration: Give God permission

Here is a prayer declaration that, if you come into agreement with it, you can use to give God permission to work in your life. Do not just read it or listen to it, but weigh what it says. Ask yourself, "Do I really want to let my guard down and override my protection mechanisms so that God can come in?" If you do want that, then pray something like this:

To stream, scan the QR code or visit the resources page.

Father, I thank You
for Your presence
around me and in me.
I thank You for this safe place
within Your love, joy and peace.
I choose to open my heart up to You.

Reveal my blind self to me.
Show me the hidden motives
of my heart.
Show me how I look
compared to Your image.
Wash me, cleanse me
with Your living words of love, joy, peace and comfort.

I stand in the light of Your truth.
I ask You to search me.
I present myself to You, Jesus, my High Priest,
as a living sacrifice.
I ask You to skin me:
remove all barriers, walls and partitions.

Remove all layers of self-righteousness;
remove all the masks that I hide behind;
remove all my defence behaviour patterns.
Remove all my coping mechanisms;
remove all my mindsets –
strongholds that I have built up
to defend my false beliefs and values.

Remove all patterns of thinking,
philosophies, ideas, lies,
values not of Your kingdom.
Remove all layers of doubt and unbelief,
Remove all my emotional layers
of rejection, insecurity, fear, and dependence.

Remove all layers of guilt and shame;
remove all layers of anger, resentment,
bitterness and unforgiveness;

> remove all layers of control, independence,
> stubbornness, rebellion, pride and self-sufficiency.
>
> Give me revelation
> of my true identity as a son.
>
> Renew my mind to the mind of Christ.
> Meet all my unmet needs in Yourself.
> Heal all my unhealed hurts.
> Restore my soul to wholeness
> by reintegrating all my parts.

Here is what you can agree to receive:

> I receive Your unconditional love,
> acceptance, affirmation and approval.
> I stand transparent and naked and unafraid before You.
> I hear You say, "I see You, and I love You."
> I receive Your value, Your esteem, and Your worth.
> I receive Your strength, patience, perseverance, courage,
> boldness, humility and confidence.

I am aware that this is a challenge, especially if you have not gone through anything like it before[23]. But consider making it a lifestyle rather than a one-time declaration. Allow God to work in you continually as you maintain an attitude of openness to His healing and transformation. If you consistently engage in this without holding back, you will come to experience a flow from the inside out, addressing and resolving the blockages that obstruct the gateways of your spirit, soul and body.

Activation #9 Cleansing Soul Gates

Now we are going to invite Jesus to enter the gateways of our soul and stand with us in those gates. Allow Him to purify, refine, open and unblock whatever is necessary to allow the free flow of His love and healing into our soul. These gateways are the connection points between our soul and spirit. If they

---

[23] Many people have found the *Transformation* series helpful. It is available from our website eg.freedomarc.org either as a standalone series or as part of an *Engaging God* subscription.

are blocked or negatively influenced, the flow from the inside out may be hindered or even shut down completely. You may find it useful to have a copy of the gateways diagram at hand.

I particularly invite you to use the audio for this activation. In the last few minutes of the recording I play crystal bowls to release particular sounds and frequencies. These carry the healing intention to release trauma within your soul, from within your conscious or subconscious memories, and from the cells of your brain and your body. As trauma is released, it can be replaced by the love, joy and peace of God.

If you cannot play the recording now, feel free to use this written version for the moment, but I recommend you listen to it later.

> Let's engage Jesus in our spirit
> through first love.
> Let's open the door.
>
> We are going to take the yoke of Jesus
> because then He can restore our soul
> as we are yoked to Him.
>
> He is going to walk us through this.
> If you don't know how to get to any
> of these gateways,
> if you yoke yourself to Jesus
> He will take you there.
>
> Do not worry about 'seeing' it –
> just allow the experience to impact you.
>
> Jesus, as the Way, Truth and Life,
> is going to lead us to each gateway of our soul.
> Jesus, as perfect love and Prince of Peace,
> will cleanse the gateways of our soul from fear.
>
> So be willing to take His yoke upon you.
> He is knocking and He wants you to open the door.

To stream, scan the QR code or visit the resources page.

So I would encourage you to close your eyes.
Picture that door.
Just by faith, reach out
and by choice, choose to open the door of first love
and welcome His presence.
Welcome Jesus, as Prince of Peace,
to come into your spirit.

And be willing to take His yoke upon you.
Choose to be yoked to Him.
Ask him to put His yoke upon you,
because His yoke is easy and His burden is light
and you will find restoration for your soul.

Ask Jesus to walk you to the gateways of your soul.
He will take you through the gates of your spirit.
He will take you to the gates of your soul.

He is going to walk you to your conscience gate.
And He is standing with you at your conscience gate –
it may need to be opened –
He is going to cast all fear, guilt, shame, condemnation
from your conscience.
And the Prince of Peace
is going to bring wholeness to your conscience.
So just let Him reveal His love,
reveal His desire to make you whole.

And Jesus will walk you to your imagination gate.
The perfect love of Jesus will cast out all fear
and cleanse all negative images and memories.
The Prince of Peace will unblock that gate
and purify your imagination,
so that you will find it easier
to receive a flow of revelation from Him.
Choose to surrender that gateway to Him.
Jesus, as the Truth, let Him reveal to you
the truth of your imagination
and its value and worth.

Let Jesus walk you to your reason gate.
Let His perfect love cast out all fear
within the way you think,
in the way your mind works.
Jesus, the Truth, let Him challenge
all wrong mindsets, belief systems,
doctrines, theology, paradigms and worldviews –
anything that is not of His kingdom,
anything which is a lie.
Let the Truth, let the Prince of Peace
bring that gateway into a new measure of wholeness,
cleansed, so truth can flow from the inside out.

Let Jesus walk you to your mind gate.
Let perfect love cast out all fear
from your conscious mind.
Let Jesus, the Truth,
challenge any lies that you're believing.
Let Jesus, the Prince of Peace,
bring you to a measure of wholeness
and enable truth to fill your conscious mind.

But also let Him into your heart,
and your subconscious mind and memories,
and let His perfect love cast out all fear
from your unconscious and subconscious mind.
And let Jesus, the Truth,
challenge any lies that you have been programmed by,
which may be lodged in your memory.
Let the truth expose the lies
and let the Prince of Peace
bring that whole measure of wholeness
to cleanse your mind,
to renew your mind so that truth can flow.

Let Jesus walk you to your emotions gate,
and let perfect love cast out fear from your emotions.
Let the truth bring healing
to the hurts and pain of rejection
that may be lodged in your memory.

And let the Prince of Peace
bring healing and wholeness to your emotions.
Let Jesus, as the Life,
begin to meet all your unmet needs
for love and acceptance and approval and affirmation.
He affirms you from the inside out
and activates this gate with life.

Let Jesus walk you to your will gate.
Let perfect love cast out all fear.
Let the Truth challenge and cast out
all doubt and unbelief
as you surrender your will,
you surrender any rebellion, stubbornness, or resistance.
Let all the barriers down
and let the Prince of Peace
bring healing and wholeness to your will.
Trusting in His love, trusting in His care,
trusting that He loves you and cares for you,
you are willing to surrender your will to His.

Now let Jesus walk you to your choice gate.
Let perfect love cast out all fear from your choices.
And let the Prince of Peace
draw you into His wholeness and love.
And as He asks you to worship Him
by laying down and acknowledging His kingship
so that you can surrender your free will choices
to only do what you see the Father doing
so that the life of heaven can flow through you;
that all your gateways will be open,
that the glory of God will purify and make you whole.
And all needs that you have
to draw from the life of the spirit in independence,
that you can surrender.
You can surrender all independence to Him.
And that peace will bring you into a place of trust.

Stay in that place of rest.

> So as Jesus is yoked to you as the Prince of Peace,
> as Jesus is the Way, the Truth and the Life,
> as Jesus is perfect love,
> Jesus is safe and secure
> and you can trust Him with your soul.
>
> Make that choice to trust Him with your soul.
> Remove any barriers,
> let down any self-protection
> and allow His healing power,
> carried on the sounds and frequencies of His love
> to make you whole.

Parts scan

As we have seen, as a result of negative experiences in our upbringing, or from trauma, we may have 'stuck' emotional parts.

> As you remain in rest,
> ask Jesus, the Truth, to show you
> if you are stuck in any area, emotionally, at any age.
> He may reveal a memory,
> or He may give you an age.
>
> As He reveals any stuck emotional parts,
> call them to come to Him.
> And let Jesus call to those parts,
> to penetrate all fear and all barriers with love.
> Call those stuck emotional parts
> to be reintegrated, to be made whole;
> to come back into wholeness, into Christ.

This might just be the beginning of a journey for you. Be assured that He will complete the work he has begun in you. Continue to engage in intimacy with Him and to ask Him to bring you into peace and wholeness, filled with His love; and this journey will continue until you come into the fullness of your inheritance as a son of God.

15. Separating and Reintegrating Soul and Spirit

God's desire for us is that we become whole, He wants to make us complete, preserving our spirit, soul and body, and sanctifying us. As we surrender our soul, it becomes apparent that we need our soul and spirit to be separated from the outside in, so that God can reintegrate them properly, from the inside out.

But we all, with unveiled face, beholding as in a mirror the glory of the Lord, are being transformed into the same image from glory to glory, just as from the Lord, the Spirit (2 Corinthians 3:18).

That image is the image of our sonship, or the image of Jesus as the Son of God. This transformation is not instant; it is a process. We move from one degree of glory to another. So, while Jesus completed the work on the cross, the renewal of our minds is ongoing. It involves continually aligning our thinking with God's thoughts about Himself and us.

Since God is infinite, our minds will need to expand to grasp His infiniteness. Our consciousness will become enlarged as we experience God in ever deeper ways, and it will never return to its previous size. This expansion changes us. Think of how a balloon stretches when inflated: let the air out and it is still larger than it was before. He wants to encounter us in such a way that it expands our consciousness and challenges us on what we thought we knew, what we do know, and what there is to know. And the more we know God, the more we realise how much more there is to know. There are always surprises around the next corner!

Learning to display the glory of God allows us to manifest our sonship on earth, as it is in heaven. Our glory reflects His glory. As we know Him more, we shine more brightly. God always desires the best for us, even though He will continue to love us whether we choose to embrace and pursue this journey or remain stagnant in our growth. Since you are still with me, I imagine you are not content to stagnate.

Search me, O God

Search me thoroughly, O God, and know my heart;
Try me and know my anxious thoughts;
And see if there be any hurtful way in me,
And lead me in the everlasting way.
(Psalm 139:23-24).

I have prayed these verses many times, and if you do so too, please be sure you mean what you say. Be prepared for God to examine you (it is for your benefit, not His). He already sees; He already knows. He loves you too much to want you to remain the same when there is so much more of your inheritance for you to receive. It is important to know by experience your identity and inheritance as a son because your assigned position of authority in the kingdom is tied to that knowledge.

Let Him examine you and reveal any hurtful ways or motives in your heart. Allow Him to lead you on the everlasting way that originates from eternity, the path He has always desired for you. Understand that God examines and reveals not just your behaviours but the motives of your heart. Painful though it has been at times, I have learned not to shy away from acknowledging them. Such motives stem from past events and decisions that have formed patterns within our hearts.

When I first began exploring my gateways, I was on a forty-day fast in 2010. On day 19 of the fast, I had an extraordinary experience where I spent hours in heaven (though it was even longer in heavenly time). When I returned, Jesus told me to listen to Ian Clayton. At that time I had never heard of him, so I did a quick Google search and came across a video entitled "Transrelocating." When I discovered he was from New Zealand, I wondered if God wanted to take me there, although I had no idea how to transrelocate. But as it turned out, Ian was in the UK, and only 70 miles from me in Torquay, that very night. He was in scattergun mode, speaking very rapidly and without much explanation on a diverse range of topics. Most of the people who came with me were baffled, but for me it was reassuring, confirming the heavenly experiences I had been having.

Afterwards, I listened to some more of his teaching, in which He described how he worked through all the gateways of his spirit, soul and body covering every year of his life (see the gateways diagram in chapter 5 or the coloured version on the resources page). I decided to follow his example: it was an emotionally draining process because I did it over a span of just three weeks, reviewing more than 50 years of my life.

As I explored my conscience gate, I asked Jesus to reveal the thoughts and motives of my heart. I began with the current year and worked backward. I discovered patterns of thinking and behaviour that I did not like at all, patterns which had developed over the years and become part of who I was. I had to accept, own, and renounce these patterns. Eventually, I identified their root causes and renounced them.

As my conscience gateway was purified and refined, the flow improved. I became more sensitive, and my conscience became finely tuned to the point where I would naturally veer away from things that did not align with my newfound clarity and sensitivity. I worked through all my gateways, using a spinner[24] based on the gateways diagram to visualise and align them all to see how the river of life flowed through each combination.

For instance, when I lined up my spirit gates of reverence and the fear of the Lord with the soul gate of conscience, my conscience was no longer just a protector against wrong actions; it began to guide me towards better ones. I became more attuned to the leading of the Holy Spirit, so that I felt His peace in my decision-making. I opened all these gates to Jesus, and for the next several years He was actively at work within me, even when I was not consciously aware of it. Sometimes, I would be given insight into a change I had noticed, but often I would just find that my thinking and

---

[24] Find instructions for making a spinner at freedomarc.blog/aligning-gates

behaviour had shifted. Still, I knew I was benefitting from whatever transformation was occurring.

Trading floors

Our programming is influenced not only by personal experiences but also by environmental factors, including unmet needs. When we lack affirmation in specific areas, we may seek to fulfil those needs in the wrong places. We may manipulate people to meet our needs, leading to dishonesty and a lack of transparency in our relationships. This can contribute to co-dependent relationships, often traceable back through generational lines.

The motives of the heart are often rooted in a desire to regain a lost wholeness. When people engage in what we might label as bad behaviours (or even 'sin'), it is an indication of a broken identity and a desperate search for something they will never find apart from God. Instead of judging and condemning them, I now recognise it as a cry for help, a desire to fill the void or pain within them.

Negative trading started with Satan before time, and it continued with Adam and Eve's disobedience. Legitimate desires of the heart are God-given and can be met by seeking wisdom from God. James distinguishes between godly wisdom which comes down from above and that which is earthly, natural and demonic. Godly wisdom enables us to partake in God's own divine nature and receive everything beneficial for us. Earthly, natural and demonic wisdom originates from Satan's desire to elevate himself, saying, "I will ascend; I will be like God." These are trading roots of self-seeking, leading to all sorts of negative consequences.

Our relationships often form around the pursuit of love or significance. God showed me how my own longing for significance stemmed from a lack of recognition from my own father, and had led me to seek significance in the eyes of others. I wanted a position within the church I attended because I believed it would gain me that recognition. The church leader exploited my eagerness, and I ended up doing all kinds of tasks for him, trading my services for the hope of being acknowledged and eventually becoming a leader myself. That all fell away when I was able to receive my significance from God. Now, I am not particularly concerned about what people think of me because I know what God thinks of me, and His opinion is the one that counts. I am not preoccupied with reputation, if I even have one. My focus is on God's perspective. Positive opinions of others can be encouraging, but they are incidental to the course of my life.

We want to avoid all pathways associated with the tree of the knowledge of good and evil, operating independently of God. The counterfeit methods we sometimes employ to gain love, acceptance, affirmation, approval, security, provision, purpose, destiny, satisfaction, fulfilment, leisure, peace and so on are all spiritually unhealthy substitutes for what God provides. They are negative trading floors which offer distorted alternatives to God's provision. I realised that I had sacrificed on many of these altars throughout my life. Even when not consciously aware of it, the motive was there, and it needed to be dealt with. Only as my spirit has been increasingly purified have these motives begun to fade away.

Such trades often come with deadly strings attached, damaging lives and relationships and creating generational patterns that can be passed down to our descendants. Familiar spirits can be involved in activating and operating these motives. The pathway of the tree of the knowledge of good and evil can seem like a shortcut to success, power, wealth, position, influence or gratification. The enemy always tempts us with the promise of immediate gain. God's way is through maturity and growth, and there are no shortcuts.

In the charismatic church, we have often promised the impartation of spiritual gifts or a particular anointing through the laying on of hands. I travelled around the world to get people to pray for me because there was supposedly a transferable anointing on offer, for the cost of the airfare and a conference ticket. Now I do not lay hands on anyone. Whilst I can certainly impart a seed to you through my testimony or teaching, I now know that we all need to cultivate our own relationship with God; and that takes time, perseverance, diligence, and desire. Personal anointing and spiritual growth come through developing a deep relationship with God, not through shortcuts or transfers. If it is not relational, it is not God; and it is not the kingdom.

The devil tempted Jesus but He was not buying it. He refused to trade into the shortcuts he offered. His victory ultimately reversed the damage caused by Adam's fall, setting us free from the need for shortcuts and trading on false altars. We call them 'trading floors' because they are places where we offer something of ourselves in return for something we desire.

These are the trading floors commonly identified, the traps that can lead us astray:

1. **Tyre**: The pursuit of money and materialism; the constant desire for more wealth and possessions.

2. **Athalia (Kingly Seed)**: The quest for power and position, entangled in the pursuit of influence and authority.

3. **Jezebel**: This involves manipulation, control, and even witchcraft; trying to dominate others and bend them to our will. It can encompass dependency and addiction.

4. **Murder**: Not actual murder, but character assassination, tearing someone down or ruining their reputation.

5. **Delilah**: Seduction, enticement by alluring temptations that may promise good things but ultimately lead us away from God's best for us.

6. **Leviathan**: Gossip, lies, and deception; causing or allowing untruths or false impressions to proliferate.

7. **Apollyon**: Apollyon opposes the gospel and keeps us from living out the good news. It is when our actions and attitudes are anything but good news to the world.

Avoiding these traps begins with allowing God to search and examine our heart. Our thoughts reveal (and sometimes determine) what is going on in our lives. What am I thinking? What am I feeling? Do I have toxic thinking? Am I holding onto anger or negativity? Am I seeking approval from external sources? Am I angry with myself? Am I feeling negative about myself? You have to be brutally honest. You cannot hide anything, especially from God, so you may as well be completely open with Him. He loves us through all of this.

I knew that. That love was my anchor when I had to face the offensive parts of myself. I had to look at every need I had, and ask whether that need was being met in God or somewhere else. Even though I had learned to let my spirit rule over my soul, it still had those motivations which it would have turned to, had my spirit allowed. I owned my motives and acknowledged them as sin (outworking of lost identity). They existed because I had a wrong image of myself. I would not have needed a position granted by a church leader if I had known my position in God. I wanted them cleansed and purified so that they would never surface again.

God refines our heart and motives, and this also extends to our heritage. Recognising these patterns in our family's history and breaking these generational chains is crucial, not least for our children. That is what the scriptures about sin being passed down to the third and fourth generation are warning about. We want to cut those ties before they affect the next generation. If I had known and dealt with all this earlier, I could have passed on a better natural and spiritual inheritance to my children. All I can do now is deal with it in me and legislate for it to be revealed to them, because once they participate in something, it becomes their responsibility to deal with it (before they also pass it on).

This is how I approached God every day in this period. I would step into heaven and come into the presence of God. It is much easier to do this in heaven and not be affected by things on earth. I would say:

Father, I thank You that You have made a way for me
to access your heavenly presence by faith.
I step in through the veil of Jesus
through the way of the cross.
I present myself to You, Jesus, my High Priest,
in surrender as a living sacrifice.
I want Your will.
I only want to choose Your will
(I knew where all my own choices had led me).

I submit to You,
the authority of the living word in my life.
I step through the veil of truth into the holy place.

I stand in the light of Your truth.
I ask You to search me,
Reveal my blind self to me.
Show me the hidden motives of my heart.
Show me the pathways of the tree of the knowledge
of good and evil that I have followed.
Show me where I have accepted Satan's deceptions.

Reveal where I have followed earthly, natural
or demonic wisdom to meet my own needs.
Show me where I have traded
by taking a shortcut to gratification
through success, money, position, influence, or power.
Show me where I have received my identity
from performance, work or ministry.
Show me where I form relationships
to meet my own needs
for love, acceptance, affirmation and approval.
Show me where I have sought to meet my own needs
through humanism or rationalism,
following the forbidden pathway of self.

I submit and surrender my life to following the pathway
of the Tree of Life as my source.
I commit myself to a lifestyle
of renouncing all negative trading.

> I renounce my sin,
> where I have followed the path of good and evil.
> I renounce the patterns of sin in my heart.
> I renounce all my defence mechanisms,
> coping mechanisms and survival methods.
>
> Give me revelation of my true identity as a son of God.
> Give me a heart secure in its identity.
> Renew my mind to the mind of Christ.
> Meet all my unmet needs in Yourself.
> Heal all my unhealed hurts.
> Restore my soul to original condition.
>
> I receive your unconditional love,
> acceptance, affirmation, and approval
> from the source of the tree of life.
>
> I stand transparent and naked.
> Skin me.
> Cut my head off.
> (I do not want my own thinking getting in the way).
> Chop off my legs.
> (I do not want to walk into places you do not want me to go).
> Split me open and reveal everything that is on the inside.

I said all that every day for about 2 years, as well as doing everything else I was doing in heaven. It was all part of my journey of being a living sacrifice, and I really meant it. And God would expose things right down to my genetic material.

But then I would have to step back into this realm to try to walk it out, because I could not stay in heaven. Later, once I was able to do so, I began to see everything I was doing in heaven continually flowing into the earth realm. The desire and the motivation of my heart to love God, to fulfil my destiny and to bring glory to Him: that is all that now motivates me here, because it is continually flowing from heaven. Stepping in and stepping out is a great starting point, but when we are out, we are not flowing from being in. To get to the point of being in and out at the same time, flowing from one to the other continually, we need the fire of God to purify our hearts, to purify our motives, because the pure in heart will see God. That was essential for me before I could venture through the dark cloud to encounter the Person of God. He would not have allowed me to come with a heart unprepared for the journey. He does not wish harm upon us; He protects us. I could not get through the cloud until my heart was at a point where I could meet Him face to face.

Look again at that gateways diagram. We have our spirit, our soul, and our body. Our spirit is where the river of life flows. Then come the gateways of our soul: our conscience, imagination, reason, mind, emotions, choice and will. Choice is the key here. You can address the issues in all the other gateways, but it is only at the point of choice that the motives behind all these mean anything.

How many times have you made New Year's resolutions that never came to anything? You might have had the desire and even planned it all out but faltered when it came to making the choice on a daily basis. Our choice is ultimately motivated by worship. Nothing to do with singing songs, worship is an acknowledgement of Jesus as the Lord of lords and the King of kings, bowing down in obeisance to Him. Worship means choosing to align yourself with the Father's will, a desire to do what we see the Father doing. I built that desire over this period by surrendering every day; and as I saw the fruit of it in my life, so the desire grew stronger.

Cutting the cords

But I had to deal with the umbilical cords that linked my soul to my spirit. In the womb, a baby is connected to its mother through an umbilical cord that provides essential sustenance. It is a natural and necessary connection. In my case, these umbilical cords were operating in reverse, driven by the wrong motivations, and I know I am not alone in that.

Now, if you have an umbilical cord running from your conscience to your fear of God and reverence gates, it can

SEPARATING AND REINTEGRATING

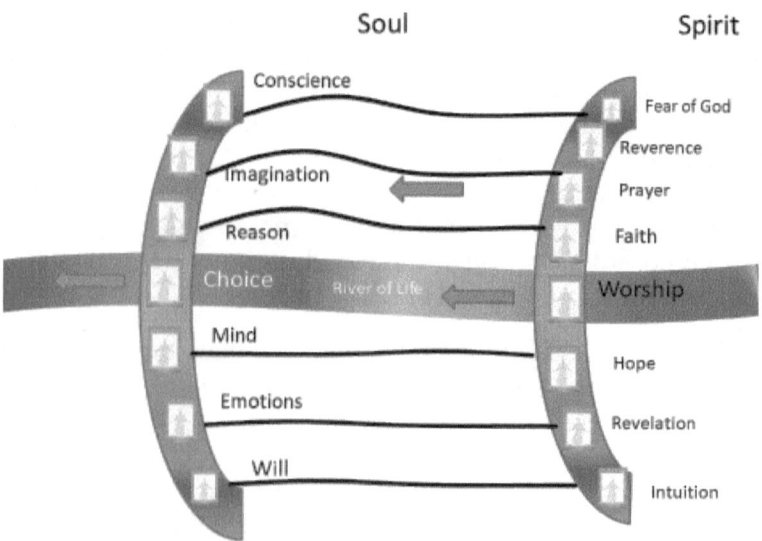

make you very legalistic. Religious spirits will turbocharge these tendencies, turning a legitimate desire for holiness into an obsession with keeping the rules. That happens when the connection is working in the wrong direction, from our soul to our spirit. Fear of God and reverence are designed to empower our conscience by working from the inside out.

I began to realise how many of these reversed connections I actually had, so I asked God to search my heart and expose anything that needed changing. He showed me that my soul had been operating independently: I was doing things for Him, but it was still about meeting my own needs. Yes, I had faith, but I was using it to feel good about myself. I had received the most awesome revelations, but I had used them for personal validation. Looking back on the four-month process, I can see the profound transformation God worked in me. I did not fully comprehend it as it happened; it was too overwhelming.

Once I began to see how many connections were misaligned, drawing from the wrong direction, of course I wanted them severed. However, I was concerned that if I cut them myself, that would only reinforce my soul's independence. So I chose to surrender and ask Jesus to take charge. He is the Word of God and the Sword of the Spirit, and well equipped for the task. He severed those cords. For me, this confirmed that I was not dependent on my own actions but reliant on Him.

The next step was to properly reconnect my soul and spirit, so that fear of God and reverence worked on my conscience, reinforcing it in a positive manner. Hope sparked visions in my imagination; and faith worked in my reason centre, causing me to believe. Intuition empowered my emotions, turning me into a sensor, picking up on subtle cues. For me, prayer operates primarily in my mind because it entails a two-way, constant communication in relationship with God. Most of my interaction with God occurs through conversing with Him in my thoughts. I operate in the realm of heaven through my thoughts: in a sense, thought is the language of heaven to me. This was how God always intended these connections to work harmoniously within us.

The rivers of living water flow from the throne of God in heaven, and He desires them to flow into us and through us. However, for this flow to take place, all the gates within us must be open. A stagnant pool, like the Dead Sea, harbours little life, because water gathers there but nothing flows out. My intention was to receive and give freely, understanding that this was not all about me; it was about sharing this life with others and about kingdom authority touching the earth.

During a conference session in Exeter with Justin Abraham, God took my heart and held it up, showing me that my valves were blocked; the issue was not with the incoming valves; it was with the outgoing ones. I had an immense capacity to receive, but there was not enough flowing outwards. God enlarged the valves, allowing a greater flow, then called me to engage with and mentor more people, which I saw was the opportunity to freely give what I had received.

The next day, back in the local church, we had a remarkable experience with the Golden River and its seven streams. It was life-transforming, one of the most powerful encounters I have had here in the earth realm. I have had more extraordinary experiences in heaven, but it was an intense experience that has had a lasting impact on me.

Some little while before, we had received a prophetic word that God wanted to pour out a Golden River. We prepared diligently and invited Him to do so on that particular Sunday. We laid out our flags, and there were seven streams flowing. As we all walked on the flags, something extraordinary happened: God moved in a deep and profound way[25]. One day after having my capacity to flow outwards supernaturally increased, God also greatly increased my capacity to receive.

Now we are going to invite Jesus into the space between our soul and spirit, and to sever those cords. This requires a genuine willingness. It is not about going through the motions; it is about truly desiring this separation. You do not need to have all the answers. If you are aware of any area where you have been drawing on your independence wrongly, confess it and surrender it. But if not, you can still surrender and express your desire for these connections to be separated.

We will ask Jesus, the living Word, the Truth, to discern and reveal any umbilical cords running from soul to spirit. Then, as the Sword of the Spirit, we will invite Him to divide our soul and spirit; to untether our spirit from our soul, liberating it from being bound to the earth. This freedom allows us to soar like eagles or fly like butterflies, living in dual realms. Then we will call upon Jesus, the Prince of Peace, to make us whole by reintegrating our soul and spirit. This quantum entanglement will empower us to live in dual realms simultaneously. Everything we are involved with in heaven can resonate and manifest instantly on earth, often without us even being consciously aware of it. It can just flow.

Embrace this transformative process to become whole, which is what God desires for each of us. As we become more and more transformed into the image of God, we will see greater

---

[25] See the postscript to my first book, *My Journey Beyond Beyond*.

authority and power released in our lives because heaven will acknowledge us as children of God. Heaven recognises our identity; but if we are not aware of it, heaven sees that too. In heaven, the angels respond differently to those who know their identity and those who do not. Your angels here on earth are actively trying to help you discover your identity. They want you to claim your inheritance, so they will work overtime to diligently support you. They have nothing to do if you do not interact with them. If your soul has been seeking recognition for its own needs, particularly in matters of affirmation or trading, allow these things to fall away.

This is a prayer with which you can come into agreement in preparation for the activation which follows it.

> I choose to surrender my soul's rights to You.
> I choose to surrender any path I have followed from the DIY tree.
> I choose to surrender all works of my soul to validate itself.
>
> I choose to surrender my redemptive gift to you.
> (You can name it if you know what it is).
> I declare I will not use it for self-validation.
>
> I ask you to untether me from being earthbound.
> Free me so that I am free to soar beyond the earth into the spiritual and heavenly dimensions.
>
> I ask You, Jesus,
> the Sword of the Spirit and the living Word of God,
> to sever any umbilical cords or ties in my soul
> that have fed off my spirit
> and give my soul power to live.
>
> I ask you to untether and separate me from any ungodly ties connected to my redemptive gift.
>
> I ask that the Prince of Peace would reintegrate
> my soul and spirit from the inside out.
> I ask that you would reconnect

SEPARATING AND REINTEGRATING

and quantum entangle my soul and spirit
so that wherever my spirit is in the spiritual realms
they will be continually connected
so that heaven can flow through me on the earth.

Now we will move on to activate that in our lives.

Activation #10 Separating and Reintegrating Soul and Spirit

Read the text below, or scan the QR code and use the audio from the resources page. If you use the audio file, please be sure to play beyond the musical interlude between the separating and the reintegrating parts of the activation. You do not want to miss the reintegration!

To stream the audio, scan the QR code or visit the resources page.

We are going to invite Jesus...
He is in us.
We have already opened the door.

I encourage you to close your eyes.
Take that declaration you just made
and now, through desire,
surrender and ask Jesus to do it.

So we invite Jesus through our spirit
to come and stand between soul and spirit
as the living word of God,
as the sword of the Spirit.

And as we surrender in worship, in adoration,
we ask you, Jesus, to stand.

We consciously surrender all ties,
and all connections from our soul to our spirit.
And we ask you to sever those umbilical cords,
those ungodly ties,
to untether us,
to separate our soul from our spirit.

So just spend some time around that. If He shows you anything you need to do specifically, see the sword of the Spirit just cutting those umbilical cords and ties within.

> Now, all that has been untethered,
> all that has been separated,
> all that has been divided...
> We just ask Jesus to reintegrate our soul and spirit;
> to make us whole
> and reconnect our soul to our spirit
> by allowing the spirit to form the connection.
>
> So we ask that the river of life,
> that the presence of God's life
> would flow through our reverence gate
> and our fear of God gate
> to our conscience;
> and reconnect and empower our conscience
> to direct us and protect us as we live every day.
>
> We ask for the river of life
> to flow through our hope gate to our imagination
> so that we can really begin
> to perceive and engage heavenly revelation
> that will become the substance of our life.
>
> Let there be a flow of the river of life
> through our prayer gate to our minds,
> so we can constantly, continually
> connect in conversation
> with a flow of communication from heaven;
> from the heart of God right into our mind
> that would empower us in our thinking,
> in our feelings, in our emotions.
>
> And let there be a flow of revelation into our life,
> touching our reason, our beliefs, our values,
> that empowers them with heavenly truth,
> with eternal revelation from the very heart of God:

SEPARATING AND REINTEGRATING

the vast sum of His thoughts revealed,
that will shape how we think.

Let there be a flow of life
connecting our faith gate to our will
that will empower us to come into agreement
with the substance of our hopes
and dreams and visions –
to begin to manifest them;
to give us the diligence, the perseverance, the patience
to continue walking through this in our lives.

Let there be life that flows
to connect our worship gate with our choice gate
that all our choices
would be inspired by our worship and surrender
to only do what the Father is doing.

Let heaven begin to flow into us
as rivers of living water,
the river of life, that crystal river,
representing the very essence of life itself
flow from heaven, flow into us and flow through us,
creating an atmosphere
of love, joy and peace around us,
filled with the very essence of heaven itself.

Let there be an increase
from ankle-deep, to knee-deep,
to waist-deep, to out of our depth:
flowing with life, bringing life wherever we go.

So, untethered from the earth,
just let Him take you to soar into the heavens,
to be free:
your spirit and soul
free to engage in the realms of heaven,
with your spirit free to stay there.

Let Him quantum entangle you
so you are continually connected
from heaven to earth through your soul.
As you are made whole,
as you cooperate, as you are in agreement,
as you resonate with heaven;
as your soul comes into agreement with your spirit,
as your spirit is in oneness with the Spirit,
you are whole:
joined to the Lord and one spirit with him.

Let Him take you beyond.
Let Him take you beyond, beyond, beyond.
Free to fly, free to be, free to do, free to go.
Living in the freedom of the manifest presence of God
and manifesting that presence
through your life onto the earth.
Just let Him take you wherever your freedom takes you.
Let Him lead you.

Some of you can go out into the stars.
Some of you will have access to places under the earth,
through the atmosphere,
to your mountains and the thrones of heaven.
Standing within the heart of God in eternity.
Engaging in the four faces of God,
standing in His name...

Let Him reconnect you to creation,
let Him reconnect you to your eternal memory
of who you were before you were here.

When you are free and untethered, there are some awesome places that He will take you, but it is a journey. Do not expect to go everywhere in one go. Keep exploring; keep allowing Him to lead you, with desire, and things will open up. The authority that you have when you are in that realm will increase and you will begin to be in tune with the light, fragrance and sounds of heaven.

16. The Bridal Chamber

This is the last of the four chambers of the heart, and it is as far as I can take you in this book. If we are to access the bridal chamber, first there will be a marriage ceremony.

Please take the time now to finish writing your *ketubah* and your marriage vows. You can use the *ketubah* as the basis for your vows; you can frame them from the perspective of your destiny, vowing to fulfil what God has called you to do; you can frame them from the perspective of love, expressing your love to Jesus as your husband. Be inspired by the Spirit. Compose something which reflects your own love for Him, your own desire and passion. They can be as short or as long as you want – this is between you and Him. Bring both *ketubah* and vows with you into your marriage ceremony, because they are the basis on which you are to be married.

Once you have your *ketubah* and vows finalised, we can begin the marriage ceremony.

The marriage ceremony

Consider where you are in your journey. You have come through significant refining experiences which will have been exactly what you needed to prepare you for what is to come. This the end of your solo journey; the beginning of a deep union with God who is Father, Son and Spirit and a bonding of the heavenly and earthly in your life. This is what He said to me:

"The time of separation, of singlehood, is nearly over. The joy of walking together in the heavenly and earthly realms will be restored. Come, fire walk with me, and new vistas and new horizons will come into view. This marriage will be a marriage consummated in fire, just as it has been prepared by fire. My bride, make yourself ready for our big day."

You have been making yourself ready as you have worked through the exercises and activations in this book. If you sense that you are still not ready, ask Him about it, and go no further until He says you are.

> You stand with your *ketubah* under the *huppah*, the covering of the Father's love, grace and mercy.
>
> In marriage, you are called to leave behind singleness and independence to embrace the divine mystic union of I AM.
>
> Marriage is a dynamic journey to discover who God (Father, Son and Holy Spirit) really is.
>
> Marriage is a continuing journey, not a destination.
>
> Marriage, like any art form, requires our active participation.
>
> This marriage will be covenanted according to the terms of your ketubah.
>
> This marriage represents the Union of Christ with His bride in the love that He has for you, His treasured possession, and the apple of His eye.

The ceremony takes place in the presence of the heavenly host. The living creatures, the seven spirits of God, your personal angels, the righteous principalities, powers and rulers, the four orders of angels of transition, the cloud of witnesses, the High Chancellors of heaven and the whole angelic canopy will act as witnesses and testators to this covenant.

This is the day

Who is this one ascending from the wilderness
in the pillar of the glory cloud?
He is fragrant with the anointing oils
of myrrh and frankincense –
more fragrant than all the spices of the merchant.

Look! It is the king's marriage carriage –
the love seat, surrounded by sixty champions.
The mightiest of Israel's host
are like pillars of protection.

BRIDAL CHAMBER

*They stand ready with swords
to defend the king and his fiancée
from every terror of the night.*

*The king made this mercy seat for himself
out of the finest wood that will not decay.
Pillars of smoke, like silver mist –
a canopy of golden glory dwells above it.
The place where they sit together
is sprinkled with crimson.*

*Love and mercy cover this carriage,
blanketing his tabernacle throne.
The king himself has made it
for those who will become his bride.*

*Rise up, Zion maidens, brides-to-be!
Come and feast your eyes on this king
as he passes in procession on his way to his wedding.*

*This is the day filled with overwhelming joy –
the day of his great gladness.*
(Song of Songs 3:6-11 TPT)

So today, with great joy, we celebrate your joining to the Lord, in the presence of the Father, to become one spirit with Him.

Commitments and vows

Jesus is asking:

> Will you marry me?
> Will you put nothing above our love?
> Will you have no other gods before Me?
> Will you leave the old and cleave to the new?
> Will you honour My Father as I honour him?
> Will you honour My Father as your sole provider?
> Will you honour your image in My Father?
> Will you cease comparing yourself to others?
>
> Will you take your place
> within the hedge of My protection

so that your authority can increase?
Will you commit yourself to be fruitful, to multiply,
to fill your spheres of authority,
overcoming all obstacles and ruling?

Will you answer creation's groan for restoration?
Will you commit to fulfilling your heavenly blueprint as a
lord, a king and a son?
Will you seek first My kingdom in righteousness?

Give Him your response. If you answer "I will," those are more than mere words; they represent a genuine commitment.

Now we can ask Him about His commitment to us: you can find your own words, or use some or all of these:

Will you be my Lord, Saviour, Friend, Healer, Deliverer?
Will you be my Transformer, Rock, Light, Life, Provider,
Protector, Shepherd, Presence, Sanctifier,
Banner of Victory, Peace and Righteousness for all time?
Will you love me for all ages to come?
Will you continue to forgive me for all ages to come?
Will you bless me for all ages to come?

Will you provide for me all that I need to fulfil my
destiny, now and for all ages to come?
Will you display your glory through me, now and for all
ages to come?
Will you include me in I AM,
the great circle of Your love,
now and for all ages to come?

Ask Him whatever your spirit prompts you to ask. There is no need to leave anything out.

And God says "We will."

Now listen to Him, and hear His vows to you.
They will probably include promises like these:

I, the Lord of Life and Light, promise to love you and keep you safe and secure in the protection of My arms.

> I promise to provide for you with the abundance of My blessing,
>
> I promise to cherish you as My treasured possession.
>
> I promise to reveal Myself to you as the lover of your soul.
>
> I promise to display you as the apple of My eye.
>
> I promise to increase My glory in you, around you, and through you.
>
> I promise to reveal you openly as a jewel from the treasure chest of My heart and display you in My own crown.
>
> I promise to bless you with a dowry of love, joy and peace, overflowing in abundance.
>
> I promise to bless you with the crown of My government and a place at my right hand.
>
> I promise to give you new rings of sonship,
> a new identity and a new name.
>
> I promise to give you a new mantle, crown, and sceptre, and a new level of authority.
>
> Do you receive these vows? (Give Him your answer).

Now, it is your turn to make your vows to God. There is no script at all here; let your heart speak. If you have vows prepared, speak them out to Him. You may find it helpful to pray in tongues by way of preparation and tuning in to the Spirit.

> (Present your vows).

Hear His response to your vows.

> We receive these vows, as heaven's Bench of Three,
> as a binding commitment between heaven and earth
> and between you and the Lord.

As Father, I pronounce you are joined to the Lord
in one spirit as bride and groom.
You are now one.
What God has joined together, let no one separate.

*This is the day filled with overwhelming joy –
the day of his great gladness.*
(Song of Songs 3:11b TPT).

Do not underestimate the pleasure of His heart in your responding to Him and your willingness to come into a deeper, more intimate relationship with Him.

The bridal chamber

We have engaged the garden, dance floor and soaking room. Now finally we have come to the bridal chamber, to the consummation, the entwining of our hearts; where we move forward into this divine union, where love finds its deepest expression.

Let's step into that place of intimacy with Him.

Activation #11 Bridal Chamber

If you are listening to the audio,
close your eyes.

By faith choose to step in
through that veil,
into His Presence.
Let Him walk with you
and come into
a place of the dark cloud
in that place of intimacy,
under the covering of His Presence.

To stream the audio, scan the QR code or visit the resources page.

Let deep call to deep.
Being joined together and becoming one spirit,
entwined in His love,
surrounded with His arms.
A place of deep peace, deep rest.

Let Him take you deeper
into the revelation of who He is –
and now the revelation
of who you are as His wife,
and all that that brings to you.

Let Him consummate that relationship
with deep intimacy
and deep revelation of His wonderful love for you.
Let Him take you deeper and deeper
and deeper into that love.
Let Him cherish you.
Let Him reveal you as His cherished possession.

Let Him unveil that wonderful relationship
that this is the beginning of
going deeper and deeper and deeper.

...

The wedding day is just the beginning of the marriage relationship, so every day you have an opportunity of engaging God in a deeper and deeper way. You can expect Him to reveal Himself and unveil Himself as you spend quality time with Him in a deeper way, as deep calls to deep.

As you go forward, He is going to reveal Himself in more and more wonderful ways, and He is going to reveal you in more and more wonderful ways.

Further resources

Books

Mike Parsons' previous book in this series, *Engaging the Father*, together with his earlier books *My Journey Beyond Beyond* (2018), *The Restoration of All Things* (2021) and *The Eschatology of the Restoration of All Things* (2022) are all available to order from local and online booksellers.

For more details or to purchase as ebooks, please visit:

> eg.freedomarc.org/books

Look out for more titles in this *Sons Arise!* series coming soon.

Other media

Engaging God: our self-paced monthly subscription programme for the Joshua Generation. For your two-week free trial visit eg.freedomarc.org/subscribe-to-engaging-god

Patreon: partner with us in taking the message of God's unconditional love, limitless grace and triumphant mercy to all His children. Become a patron at patreon.com/freedomarc to join Mike and other patrons for monthly group Zooms, exclusive and early-access videos and other benefits.

Mike's YouTube channel: new videos are normally posted daily. View and subscribe at freedomarc.org/youtube

Sons of Issachar blog: shorter written articles drawn from Mike's teaching and online conversations. Find out more at eg.freedomarc.org/blog (where there are links to our blog sites in French, Spanish, Portuguese and German too).

Social media: follow Freedom ARC at

> freedomarc.org/facebook
> freedomarc.org/instagram
> freedomarc.org/pinterest
> freedomarc.org/twitter

Scripture quotations

Unless otherwise noted, scripture quotations are taken from the (NASB®) New American Standard Bible®, Copyright © 1960, 1971, 1977, 1995, 2020 by The Lockman Foundation. Used by permission. All rights reserved. www.lockman.org

Other Bible versions used

Mirror: The Mirror Bible. Copyright © 2017, 2021 by Francois Du Toit. Used by kind permission of the author. All rights reserved. app.mirrorword.net

MLV: Modern Literal Version. © Copyright 1999, 2016 by G. Allen Walker, Co-Editor. Used by permission. All rights reserved worldwide. www.modernliteralversion.org

NIV: Scripture quotations taken from The Holy Bible, New International Version® NIV®. Copyright © 1973, 1978, 1984, 2011 by Biblica, Inc.™. Used by permission. All rights reserved worldwide.

NKJV: Scripture taken from the New King James Version®. Copyright © 1982 by Thomas Nelson. Used by permission. All rights reserved.

TPT: Scripture quotations marked TPT are from The Passion Translation®. Copyright © 2017, 2018, 2020 by Passion & Fire Ministries, Inc. Used by permission. All rights reserved. ThePassionTranslation.com.

Image acknowledgement

The sunrise image used on the back cover is copyright Błażej Łyjak via 123RF Stock Photo. Used by permission.

www.ingramcontent.com/pod-product-compliance
Lightning Source LLC
Chambersburg PA
CBHW020354170426
43200CB00005B/162